Praise for
KAREN ELIZABETH GORDON

"Eerily sensitive to the creative potential of language, Karen Elizabeth Gordon has birthed a genre and renewed the language."
—Robert Grudin

"Karen Elizabeth Gordon does in words what Edward Gorey does in drawings: she presents a neat, mandarin order that can't keep out—indeed, almost invites—intrusions of the bizarre."
—*Newsweek*

"I can think of no one whose life and language would not be brightened by any and all of Gordon's work." —*Baltimore Sun*

"Gordon's books are compassion-filled little lighthouses among language's treacherous shoals." —*Sacramento Bee*

"The chief delight in Gordon's work is not so much the information she imparts . . . Rather it is in watching as she rubs words together to conjure wildly imaginative and cleverly suggestive sentences." —*Los Angeles Times Book Review*

"How rare it is to laugh as one studies a grammar text."
—Doris Grumbach, National Public Radio

"Let Ms. Gordon rewrite all the school textbooks and we'll have the most literate population in the world." —Charles Simic

"Miss Gordon manages to make the period, question mark, exclamation point, comma, and semicolon sound friendly instead of forbidding . . . Such sentences might make the Edwardian Brothers Fowler blush and, perhaps, Professor Strunk and Mr. White wince." —*New York Times*

"Gordon's saucy crash courses are short on pedantry and long on wit." —*Virginian-Pilot*

The New Well-Tempered Sentence

A Punctuation Handbook for the Innocent, the Eager, and the Doomed

Karen Elizabeth Gordon

A MARINER BOOK
Houghton Mifflin Company
Boston   New York

FIRST MARINER BOOKS EDITION 2003

For information about permission to reproduce selections from
this book, write to Permissions, Houghton Mifflin Company,
215 Park Avenue South, New York, New York 10003.

Visit our Web site: www.houghtonmifflinbooks.com.

Library of Congress Cataloging-in-Publication Data

Gordon, Karen Elizabeth.
The new well-tempered sentence : a punctuation handbook
for the innocent, the eager, and the doomed : Karen
Elizabeth Gordon. — Rev. and expanded.
p.   cm.
Rev. ed. of : The well-tempered sentence. 1983
Includes index.
ISBN 0-395-62883-0
ISBN 0-618-38201-1 (pbk.)
1. English language — Punctuation.   I. Gordon, Karen Elizabeth.
Well-tempered sentence.   II. Title.
PE 1450.G65 1993
428.2 — dc20   93-18454
CIP

Book design by Anne Chalmers

Printed in the United States of America

QUM 10 9 8 7 6 5 4 3

Several quotations in this book are from works translated into English:
Osip Mandelstam, *The Noise of Time*. Translated by Clarence Brown. Princeton University Press, 1965.
Henri Michaux, *Miserable Miracle*. Translated by Louise Varèse. City Lights Books, 1956.
Yury Olesha, *No Day Without a Line*. Translated and edited by Judson Rosengrant. Ardis Publishers, 1979.
Raymond Queneau, *The Bark Tree*. Translated by Barbara Wright. New Directions, 1971.
Silvia Monrós-Stojaković, "The Fourth Side of the Triangle." Translated by Krinka Petrov. 1990.

The illustrations come from the following sources (all are Dover Publications): Filippo Bonanni, *Antique Musical Instruments and Their Players;* Ali Dowlatshahi, *Persian Designs and Motifs;* Max Ernst, *Une Semaine de Bonté;* Jean-Ignace-Isidore Gerard (Grandville), *Fantastic Illustrations of Grandville;* Konrad Gesner, *Curious Woodcuts of Fanciful and Real Beasts;* Carol Belanger Grafton, *Love and Romance* and *Treasury of Animal Illustrations from Eighteenth-Century Sources;* Jim Harter, *Animals; Hands; Men; Women; Harter's Picture Archive for Collage and Illustration;* Richard Huber, *Treasury of Fantastic and Mythological Creatures;* Ernst and Johanna Lehner, *Picture Book of Devils, Demons, and Witchcraft*.

This book also contains illustrations from the following sources: Nick Bantock, Ta Fin Lighthouse, copyright © 1992 by Nick Bantock; Johann Georg Heck, *The Complete Encyclopedia of Illustration*, copyright © 1979 by Park Lane, Crown Publishers, Inc.; Helen Iranyi, *Book of Animals*, copyright © 1979 by The Main Street Press; Simca Moonbach by Barrie Maguire, copyright © 1992; Moon-stroked water spirit by Drago Rastislav Mrazovac, copyright © 1988; Max Ernst, *The Hundred Headless Woman (La Femme 100 têtes)*, English translation copyright © 1981 by Dorothea Tanning. Reprinted by permission of George Braziller, Inc.

Contents

Introduction

SINCE IT FIRST appeared in 1983, *The Well-Tempered Sentence* has led a life of such consummate conviviality with its readers that it began roaring over its parentheses and quotation marks, clacking its commas like castanets, and arching its back so lasciviously that it broke its own spine. What could I do but give it a new body and indulge its rage to live? There were other signs that something was afoot. Characters in the first edition started taking off their clothes, throwing masked balls, sending insinuating letters to cellists, divas, and Eurobankers, and swapping gossip and braggadocio with the beasts and voluptuaries of *The Deluxe Transitive Vampire*. To top off these taunts, the punctuation marks themselves were stirring up trouble and inviting raffish comrades in for drinks, hanging out in hotel lobbies and cities that didn't even exist back when the dummy in diamonds and furs, rummaging for her opera glasses, found a ticket to Ljubljana via Martinique.

What has happened, you see, is that along with new characters like Nimbo Moostracht, Amaranthia, and Jespera

Trost, we are introducing apostrophes and slashes. Italics have arrived in the same boat with Marina, Marimba, and some homeopathic penguins. And more than one boat is called for: the inundation that soaked several characters in the first edition has become a source of waterways and intimations from Amplochacha to the ends of the earth.

Defying the musical allusion of its title, *The New Well-Tempered Sentence* is not exactly rolling in pianos, nor is it about having a manicure before pouncing on one. There's a lot more at play here than notes and keyboards. Apparitions drift and hover; a mannequin both beast and human bounds in and out of sight; a water sprite swaps stories with a colleague from the river Styx. Relatives arrive unannounced from a dubious monarchy, while several new countries have opened their borders to rivers and refugees. A prima ballerina comes on with smoke and mirrors, and it's not only the lithe and supple taking us in for a spin: the mastodons also are at dancing school. While they learn their fox trots and entrechats (avoiding an assortment of felines never before on display), Too-Too LaBlanca does a kick at the end of a clause, showing a little slip.

Every word carries a pack of punctuation marks in its pocket to attach wherever and whenever needed in its exciting, unpredictable life. Virtuoso use of this motley collection is as enhancing to your writing as a full-spectrum vocabulary and a snazzy grammar to keep it in. In writing, punctuation fills in for the clues we receive face to face. The rakish slash cries, "Give me ambiguity or give me death!" The promiscuous hyphen is game for liaisons with anyone. A period can pirouette and still make its point. An exclamation mark leaps onto the page in the place of flaming eyes, thumping fist, a defiant thrust of chin. Come-hither/go-away looks and clandestine winks can also be conveyed after you've been at this for a while.

However frenzied or disarrayed or complicated your thoughts might be, punctuation tempers them and sends signals to your reader about how to take them in. We rarely give these symbols a second glance: they're like invisible servants in fairy tales — the ones who bring glasses of water and pillows, not storms of weather or love. Even in this book starring the marks of punctuation, their presence is more felt than seen. It's the words that will capture your eyes, enticing them to dally and glisten. One quick blink and you've caught the comma's or slash's or hyphen's message, or huddled in a parenthetical clasp. Their accomplishments are no less astonishing for occurring in a flash. What else do they remind me of? Not fireflies — too flamboyant for their everyday life. But they do stir memories of two talented young fleas I saw one summer evening in Copenhagen's Tivoli Gardens: a girl flea in pink tutu, and her brother/partner in boxer shorts, pulling a miniature cart. Like these well-trained prodigies, punctuation marks can exceed your expectations, even defy belief.

The door flies open and abruptly you are inside. The book is about to begin! A rapping sound, then scurrying and scuffling noises come from within. From faraway rooms, a cough, a moan, an indiscreet, rumpled laugh. A veranda rattles, a water pipe shudders, and a drawer is heard to slam. Somewhere a petticoat is being smoothed down. There are so many characters to compose themselves, to freeze in mid-sentence, as if you have strayed into a story already in full swing. And these *are* stories, in their small totalities: there is no want of drama here!

Someone has obviously been the houseguest of Rosie and Nimrod, but who was it that misbehaved? What word follows "darling" during that spelling lesson of hyphenated pedagogical passion? What is Tropo Gallimauf after in his granny's velvet vault? Does the name Too-Too LaBlanca refer to the white keys of a piano?

Loona, pacing hypnotically through some cloak-and-dagger or existential histrionics, is quite aware of the state of waiting she's in, but does she know what for? The tiptoe pose tilting toward some unseen horizon cannot be held for long. An out-of-doors setting can be conjectured for her impatience, or a very drafty chamber, anyway, to account for her windblown beauty — or is she simply disheveled? Have her toes turned blue with her lips in this frozen vigilance? She has not yet succumbed to despair; there's too much rapture in her face.

These and other questions must remain unanswered or be further explored by you, the reader, whose stories they also are. Oh, I am so eager to entrap you in these pages, I can barely speak!

The New

Well-Tempered

Sentence

The Exclamation Point!

WHAT A WILD, reckless, willful invention! How could we possibly live without it! Who needs words when we have this flasher! Don't you dare use it with visitors from other countries! Or with people you've only just met! Shameless behavior! Rapid heartbeats, faster breathing! Exultant whoppings!

An exclamation point begins with the writer's emotions and intentions, and demands that the reader feel them too. Its overuse has been discouraged, castigated as schoolgirlish, sophomoric, bodice ripping, puerile, purple prose, *infra dig*. Yet some writers have used exclamation points with panache, elevated them to lofty immortality: Friedrich Nietzsche, Andrei Codrescu, Laurence Sterne. They do come in handy when one is at a loss for words, or when one has the words but wants to give them added bite, whack, fire. The English language is so expressive that the right words, especially verbs, rarely need this extra blare. I've noticed when I share a few words of another's language, or vice versa, or in other cases of limited vocabulary, exclamation marks tumble in to fill the gaps, sending a valentine, an enthusiasm, or a threat from one heart to another — very direct.

The intensity that an exclamation point carries may be alarm, thrilled anticipation, thrilled enjoyment of the moment, thrilled hindsight. Or anger, admonition, astonishment, hilarity, or tenderness carried to extremes.

✐ AN ! CONVEYS:

♦ Loud noises and sudden actions:

Wham! Bang! Thwack!

♦ Apology:

Whoops!

♦ Endearment:

My baby! My joy! My heart!

♦ Reproach:

Not one pretty scrap of consideration!

♦ Menace:

Watch your step, buddy!

I'll see you in court!

♦ A surprise discovery:

You're really something!

♦ Indignant wisdom or wise indignation:

I wasn't born yesterday!

♦ Supplication:

Spare my life and save my misery!

It's obvious! In all these exclamations, it's still the words themselves saying a lot very quickly; the exclamation marks speed the process, turn up the volume, and signal to the reader in one rapid eye movement that it's urgent, heartfelt, etc. One exception is in comic books, where characters think in balloons, which sometimes are filled with unaccompanied exclamation marks, for the reader to interpret as befits the unfolding, staccato plot.

❧ An exclamation point also revs up these, among other, messages:

♦ Protest:

Oh, no! Not another one of your hairy friends!

♦ Name-calling:

You filthifier of English dreams!

♦ An ! can thumpingly round out a riveting dressing-down:

And don't you dare set foot in my hearse ever again!

♦ Irony, dread, astonishment:

What a surprise to find you here alone!

What governance lies in a well-versed tongue! What jeopardy for me!

I mean, this is not the approving nod of a nincompoop!

Was I ever crestfallen!

How exciting to see you in traction again!

What a swell soirée this has turned out to be!

What a swell soirée this has turned out to be!

❧ A pronouncement on someone's or something's qualities can be mild, with a period:

> What dejected dahlias.

❧ Or bowled over, with an exclamation point:

> What cumbersome biceps!

❧ Exclamation points make splendid companions in verbless sentences.

> And his mother, too!
> His very own flesh and blood!
> How about that!

❧ An interrogatory sentence or challenging question that is more exclamatory than inquisitive ends with one of these: !

> How did you pour your big body into that paper airplane!
> Where did a mere slip of a girl like you learn to chat up mastodons!

The exclamation mark is so familiar to us that we don't even recognize as imperative some of the sentences it's intensifying. "Let 'er rip! Fancy that! Bear with me! Let me tell you all about it!" All commands, but hardly as imperious or brutal as "*Fetch* my spats!" or "Buzz off!"

❧ Here, too, an invitation to contemplation is an imperative exclaimed:

Imagine his chagrin on discovering that Frangipani was only a wide-eyed tailor's dummy abandoned in the baron's back room!

❧ I leave you to your quiet enjoyment of the scenes that might give rise to these rousing requests:

Stop acerbating me!

Go froth and mortify!

Give me ambiguity or give me death!

Begone, foul water sprite, and take your panties with you!

❧ With the right words, or sounds, exclamation points can deplore, decry, bewail:

Arrgh! Aie! Nnff!

Oh, brave new world! Oh, ravaged inner cities!

Oh, gaping, hungry eyes! Oh, crack clouds, guns, and knives! Oh, trampled, broken lives!

❧ With exclamations, you can speak to your lord:

Oh, hear me, Gospodin!

❧ Like the question mark, the exclamation point can cascade into a series within a sentence and beyond for dramatic effect.

They took his picture! his cello! his private persona! his white roses from the grande dame in the box!

I completely lost my mind! After that I lost my dignity! my chutzpah! my sweetheart! my golden curls!

🖎 When it belongs to the quoted or parenthetical material in a sentence, an exclamation point goes inside the quotation marks, parentheses, or brackets.

> He swung her 'round, hiccupped "Eehaw!" and tossed his briefcase into her lunch.

> "You uxorious lummox!" the woman bellowed in response to his muffled pleas.

> "I can hardly believe my eyes!" he ejaculated at the canyon's edge.

> Then he stroked my nose (I tell you, he really does love me!), and he mumbled into my cleavage, and suddenly burst into tears.

🖎 In Spanish, the exclamation point comes before the sentence, inverted, as well as after it, right end up.

> *¡Qué triángulo mágico!*
> *¡Qué gaucho geométrico!*

The
Question
Mark

꘎ The question mark is used after a direct question.

Where have you been that's interesting enough to send you home like this?

Is this going to put a wonderful smudge forever upon my name?

Who's taking the money at the door? And how shall I dress not to seem real?

Warum sprach Zarathustra?

What's on your schedule to ruin today?

Hey, what's with you guys?

"Who is the captain of this capsized soul?"

Why am I reading this?

Did the debutante have an alibi the night of the pizza chef's demise?

Are you assigning too much significance to the dance card tied to his wrist?

Why did I look up *rhapsodize* in the phone book?

Who's the big cheese around here?

How can I get in your way when you don't even have one?

✺ The question mark expresses editorial uncertainty.

Saint Fracas (456?–458) had a short but raucous childhood.

✺ A question mark can turn a declarative or imperative sentence into an interrogative one.

You don't mind playing croquet in the mud?

You call that disgusting display of suburban vernacular a bon mot?

You're not mad?

✺ A question mark concludes a confirmatory question.*

You're part of that rodent family from Palermo, aren't you?

You had something else on top of all that champagne, didn't you?

✺ A request or order surreptitiously or politely phrased as a question does not end in a question mark.

Will you pardon my shabby getup and ravish me again.

---

*See Comma chapter.

Since when did the sum of two legs produce
an isosceles heart.

· 10 ·

Won't you please stop making such a private spectacle of yourself.

Would you please muffle your little commotion and straighten out your mugs.

Will you take your lummoxy feet off my uncle's ottoman, and my auntie's chin strap off your Doberman.

ɔ⊰ With rhetorical questions, a question mark is optional — at the rhetorician's discretion.

"Since when did the sum of two legs produce an isosceles heart." — Paul Aaen Gordon

How old were you when your nanny dropped you off with the wolves?

How do you *think* I got from point A to point B in a mournful, drunken lifeboat!

So what.

ɔ⊰ Question marks help speculations chime away in the reader's mind, echoing your own.

Why couldn't she breeze into a room and kick off her espadrilles like other girls? Would she never be able to wash her socks at the village fountain in the morning while the housefronts were being scrubbed, or see her own translucent toenails like seashells in the sun? What must it feel like to slide her soles along fresh white sheets, or to twitch her toes beneath the covers in the afterglow of love?

— *The Red Shoes*

ɔ⊰ An indirect question states the substance of a question without using the exact words. Another way to say this is that it reports on, not quotes, a question, and often with the help of words such as *if* and *whether,* along with the usual *how, who, what, where.*

♦ Direct:

> The duke wasn't asking, "Who stole the tarts?" but "Are there any more macaroons?"

♦ Indirect:

> The duke wasn't asking who stole the tarts, but if there were more of the macaroons.
>
> Odious flogged our flagging spirits after asking whether we would object.
>
> They asked the disheveled debutante if she'd left the riverbank at any time after walking out on the dance.

৹✤ You may come upon a question mark in the most intimate places — midsentence, for instance, and with others of its kind, ganging up on some innocent situation and interrogating it to death. Sprinkling question marks so liberally within a sentence, with no capital letters to make you think you've left it, emphasizes or mimics the thought process where such a series is appropriate.

> Are the rats rapacious? friendly? chic? Like their distant relatives in New York City, do they make nests of dollar bills? other paper money? theater programs? memos from heads of state?
>
> Is the taiga everything you were hoping for? Is it pure? distant? sublime? Are the musk oxen still in their winter coats? Are they talking to themselves? to the BBC audiences? to us?
>
> Is it on to the tundra next?

Do you love me truly? madly? deeply? Can you live without me? happily? despondently? just barely? Are we engaged? enamored? crushed? acquainted? Will you go to the ends of the earth with me? to the ball? to the mall?

ɔ❧ When a title ending with a question mark appears within a sentence, the mark remains right where it belongs, while the rest of the sentence unfurls after it, arriving in its own sweet time at its full stop, period, conclusion.

Do Androids Dream of Electric Sheep? is the book on which Ridley Scott's film *Blade Runner* is based.

ɔ❧ Only when the question mark is part of quoted or parenthetical material does it go inside quotation marks, parentheses, or brackets.

Do you agree with Proust that "each of us finds lucidity only in those ideas which are in the same state of confusion as his own"?

"Are you," they wondered, "selling tickets to a season of wayward sopranos?"

"What is life, anyway, but a pirouette in search of an ashtray?" read the prima ballerina's endorsement of the Tobacco and Other Strange Substances Consortium.

The last time I'd seen him (how long *had* it been?), he was a fugitive in a sea-blue bus.

ɔ❧ A question mark should stay at the end of an interrogative sentence that is part of another sentence.

How had this dreadful suspicion arisen? was every-one's question in that tense saloon.

We were still pondering the eternal question, Was the Big Bang an act of passion or the Freudian slip of an arrogant fool? when the storms and floods began.

⊃❖ In Spanish, an inverted question mark comes before the interrogatory sentence, and an upright one comes after it.

¿Qué tal, Pepe?

The Period

A PERIOD IS the closing mark for declarative sentences, mildly imperative sentences, and verbless sentences that are not questioning or exciting.

❧ DECLARATIVE

I give you my solemn hearsay.

Daedalus and Ariadne were both in on the labyrinth.

There were never enough bodies around for all the souls wanting to jump into them.

I won't take this sitting down.

The room filled up with philanderers, all seeking some buxom relief.

I think we've reached the flash point.

Time is the mother and mugger of us all.

I don't want to go on one of those displeasure cruises.

We have just begun to explore the possibilities of the next disaster.

IMPERATIVE

❧ We sometimes phrase our demands as requests that have the structure but not the inflection or generosity of a question. In other instances, we downshift from blatant coercion to phrase our desires or expectations, dropping off an exclamation mark in the process, and some blood pressure, too.

Don't be cruel.

Hold your horses.

I don't want to go on one of those displeasure cruises.

Come here, you little rascal.

Will you kindly slam the door in that persona non grata's face.

Watch your big bad mouth.

Let us settle our indifferences.

Will you sign this check with the scoutmaster's name.

ɔ⚜ Verbless sentences are ubiquitous in our conversations, and appear often in our writing — not only in writing meant to mimic how we actually talk. Periods are certainly one way to signal the end of such an utterance, or the end of a dialogue.

Back in a mo.

Really now.

This way to the petites.

His own mother, too.

And last, but not in the least, to my wife, for her helpful suggestions and her ontological questions.

ABBREVIATIONS

ɔ⚜ A period follows many abbreviations that stand for a single word.

Prof. Anita Hill, Ph.D.

Mrs. Curly Gallimauf

Mr. Bojangles

ms.

✺ The trend, however, is toward eliminating periods in abbreviations that refer to measurements.

lb or lb.	mph or m.p.h.
oz or oz.	mpg or m.p.g.
hr or hr.	yd or yd.

✺ You'll find myriad other sorts of abbreviations galloping across our civilization, often capitalized and rarely encumbered with periods.

♦ Organizations:

NATO, NASA, YWCA, CORE, AFL-CIO, AMA, IRA, ABA, PLO, NAACP, NEA, GSA

♦ Computers, weapons, and other technology:

RAM, CD/ROM, K, CPU, MIRV, AWACS

♦ Tests:

IQ, SAT, GRE, LSAT, MMPI, GMAT, MRI

♦ Titles:

VP, MP, CEO, MVP, CPA, DA, WPC

♦ Same goes for radio stations, and television stations or networks:

KXPR, KXJZ, NPR, BBC, C-SPAN, PBS, KCET, KQED, MTV, WETA

♦ And medical terminology:

TB, STD, MS, AIDS, PMS, VD, HIV, CPR, DOA, SIDS, IUD

Many of these acronyms have become so prevalent that we no longer know or even wonder what the letters stand for.

❧ A period follows numerals and letters in a list.

1. camels
2. dromedaries

a. Herzegovina
b. Slovenia

❧ No period is needed after a letter standing for a person's or object's name or moniker.

Exhibit B shows the faun's hoofprints on the night of the coming-out ball.

Mr. Z dodged questions left and right till one landed in his borscht.

❧ Don't use a period at the end of a sentence that is part of another sentence.

The rage and irony in his voice (I could hardly fail to notice the scorn with which he addressed me) alternated with a solicitous smile.

Le Beau's remonstrance, "You are always late and unwelcome besides," made her apologize and cry.

❧ Periods belong inside parentheses or brackets enclosing an independent sentence. If the enclosure is part of a larger sentence, the period is placed outside the parentheses or brackets. Periods go within quotation marks.

They were curled up beside their radio listening to Gustav Mahler's "I'm Gonna Lock My Heart."

We're going to dance our socks off to Presley's "Blue Suede Shoes."

We were hard at work on the second revision when Samuel slapped my face. (He had shown such irrational devotion to his own opinions before.)

Pouring her peignoir over her bored shoulders, she harrumphed, "My God, what a somnolent suite of nocturnes that was" (and what a very voluptuous drowsiness is to follow, she added to herself as she pressed his dressing gown upon him and feigned a languorous yawn).

She said, "I have just finished writing 'The Treacherous Bend in the Rainbow.'"

ɔ✤ Periods convene to create ellipses, implying missing words, trailing-off thoughts, passing time, hesitation . . . to be continued. . . . See Ellipses chapter.

The

Comma

A COMMA IS a delicate kink in time, a pause within a sentence, a chance to catch your breath. A curvaceous acrobat, it capers over the page. A comma keeps apart two words, or bits of thought, that would confuse if they touched. Some of the instances calling for commas are inflexible, and the only way to get around them is to find another way to state and arrange your ideas. Other uses, though, are intended to make the reader's experience easier, and are up to the writer's discretion or whim.

The comma is used to link and at the same time separate independent clauses of equal value that are short and have no commas within them.

> He shot pool, he drank Anchor Steam beer, and he rarely went home.
>
> He howled, he flailed, he groaned.
>
> She strutted, she sizzled, she slunk.

∝❧ An independent clause makes sense by itself and could stand as a separate sentence. It is more likely to be called an independent clause when it's part of a longer sentence. Two grammatically equivalent independent clauses may be linked by a coordinating conjunction like *and* or *but* or *or.*

I fondled his lapel.

I fondled his lapel, and I caressed his socks.

☞ The independent clause *I fondled his lapel* stands alone in the first example and is joined by another independent clause, *I caressed his socks,* in the second.

∝❧ A comma comes between two independent clauses joined by coordinating or correlative conjunctions, such as *and, but, or, nor, neither, yet, for,* or *so.* The sentence resulting from this fusion is called a compound sentence.

I haven't done it yet, so I don't think I could do it again.

Their admiration was mutual, and so was their hidebound lust.

The suspect removed his grimy white gloves, but another pair lurked beneath.

There was no outside to sit in, so we stood around looking askance.

Either I've been missing something, or nothing has been going on.

You crossed my mind, but you didn't stay there.

The left-handed members of the board were banging their soup spoons, and the agenda was engulfed by their roars.

I won't rise to the occasion, but I'll slide over to it.

He told her he belonged to another, yet his pajamas clung to her tights.

We sat waiting for some epiphany, but only a foghorn broke through the silence and encroached on the monotony of our crouching figures.

He was in it for the money, and she was looking for kicks.

ᴐ❧ Two short independent clauses joined by *and* can get along without a comma — unless the words involved would be confusing otherwise, as we'll see later in this chapter.

He wanted cash and she wanted thrills.

You tell me and we'll both know.

ᴐ❧ When the subject is stated only once, but has two actions, or verbs, a comma may help bridge them if the conjunction between them is *but:*

She always carries bandages with her, but will give them only to bleeding people to whom she has been formally introduced.

ᴐ❧ In situations like these, where two or more verbs have the same subject and are joined by *and*, no comma is necessary.

She woke up and gave the world a hurt look.

We slipped off into the forest and made love under a terrible apprehension.

Eat your cake and make it too.

She unfurled her umbrella in the dark and muttered obscenities into its awful folds.

He pressed her fragrant fingertips to his lips and remorselessly told her the hideous truth.

Her bejeweled puissance quivered across the foyer and set the ushers to quaking in their boots.

⊃✦ Occasionally, for special effect (e.g., tumbling, running away), three or four such verbs can gallop along with the same subject—even a compound one.

Alyosha and Jean-Pierre scrubbed their teeth and practiced mugging and touched up their hairdos and horns.

At this very moment, a deep discussion of clauses and phrases is taking place in *The Deluxe Transitive Vampire*, should you be desperate or ardent to know more. But you may also take it from me that independent clauses are those able to stand alone as sentences, although they are often linked together in one way or another within the same sentence. Dependent clauses, although they possess both noun and verb (subject and predicate), are not self-sufficient in that way, mostly because of the linking word (a relative pronoun or subordinate conjunction usually) that, in cahoots with the dependent clause, is looking for an independent clause with which to form an attachment. Sentences are born of this mating dance, as the following examples illuminate. We'll consider adverbial dependent clauses first. Adjective clauses, which modify nouns and pronouns, await us around a few curves of commas and the road.

⊃✦ A comma is needed after a dependent clause, usually a fairly long one, that precedes an independent clause.

If you'll let out the cat, I'll let out the last word.

When it became apparent that they were just pulling our legs, we started kicking.

As far as I'm concerned, all phone calls are obscene.

Once we have these mastodons under control, we'll bring on the incense and the priests.

If you'll let out the cat, I'll let out the last word.

After he painted her face and knees, they sauntered into the lugubrious crowd.

When I last saw him, in that sea-blue bus, he was scattering glass beads behind him as he fled.

Once the deluge had passed, and while we were still drying our socks over some hot coals, we exchanged confidences about our most secret possessions that had been torn from our rooms by the water.

✧ A restrictive dependent clause (a clause that would alter the meaning of the main clause if omitted) that follows a main clause should not be set off by a comma.

Torquil and Jonquil plotted their tryst *so it would fall on Epiphany.*

I will accompany you to the spa *if we can go hear Ornette Coleman afterward.*

They sauntered out among the masked carousers *after he painted her face and knees.*

We'll bring on the incense and priests *once we have these mastodons under control.*

✧ Adverbial phrases and clauses are usually accompanied by a comma or two, depending upon their placement in a sentence. An adverbial phrase beginning a sentence is often followed by a comma.

Once the deluge had passed, and while we were still drying our socks over some hot coals, we exchanged confidences about our most secret possessions that had been torn from our rooms by the water.

From the right, the moon rises like a proud tangerine.

Before stepping out, Charmiane locked the last remaining secret drawer.

Because of this baffling situation, we all gave up and adjourned to a nearby bar.

In these laconic gestures, she conveyed the story of the creation, the history of the world, and a prognosis for the ensuing millennium.

After these inclement outbursts, he sends tulips, charwomen, and folding chairs.

After this string of scurrilous anecdotes, she sprinkled the lawn with pearls.

✺ But the comma is often omitted after short introductory adverbial phrases.

At dawn the sun began to rise.

At vespers we usually raise our voices aloft.

At breakfast we consumed a reprehensible smorgasbord of assorted Nordic things.

In your pockets you are fumbling with the keys to a strange place.

✺ When an introductory adverbial phrase appears immediately before the verb it modifies, no comma is required because the relationship is clear.

Out of the bushes appeared a well-dressed man with his head underneath his arm.

Into the circle of blind conformists leaps a dissident shining with woe.

In these laconic gestures, she conveyed the story of the creation,
the history of the world, and a prognosis for
the ensuing millennium.

In the hallway danced a bevy of folk-struck maidens with flowers and snakes in their hair.

Out of this domestic chaos emerged a placid and reso-lute truce.

Dragging travelers from their troikas was a pack of wolves with sheep's voices.

🪡 A comma comes before and after an adverbial phrase or clause occurring in the middle of a sentence between the subject and the verb.

The little orchestra, before treating us to an evening of scabrous melodies, stuffed themselves with snails.

Georgia, after lifting her petticoats, turned the corner in her clattering heels.

Mitzi, in a manner that surprised everyone present, broke into a hefty aria and then proceeded to swallow a sword.

The goat, after eating her lederhosen, started in on her Dürrenmatt.

🪡 In their own realm, adjective clauses are every bit as en-hancing as adverbial phrases and clauses. They come with two different purposes in mind: restrictive and non-restrictive. A restrictive clause, as its name announces, actually changes or specifically modifies the subject or object it identifies. As intrinsic as such a clause or phrase is to the sentence's meaning, then, no commas cut it off from the noun or pronoun it belongs with.

The guys *who are bald* are made to sit on the south side of the room.

Troika attacker with plenty of time to study ethics and think things over.

These liner notes *by Peter Guralnick* are setting the Elvis record straight.

The Renaissance man *who built those castles in the air* is now back in his labyrinth.

Other fortresses *under his jurisdiction* have never sought clemency for March hares.

Anyone *who disagrees with me* had better step forward and explain his recalcitrance at once.

All laughter *that is out of place* will be stuffed into a nearby drawer.

Everyone *who has a weak instep* must dance the tarantella in stocking feet.

The author *who wrote about a moocow coming down the road* also wrote of kissed breasts all perfume.

The ruffians *who are wearing chintz* were left in the hallway to think it over.

⌘ Nonrestrictive phrases and clauses giving descriptive information *not* essential to the meaning of the sentence are set off by commas.

The engineer, *who was asleep at the time,* missed the apparition floating past the windows of the train.

The interloper, *whom we had to suppress,* was given a ticket to Tangier.

Raymond, *who usually wears overalls,* showed up in a green kimono.

The final act of the play, *which was unevenly hilarious,* took place on a drifting barge.

After a day's hike through torrid regions of my own body, I arrived at a small oasis manned by a dead

The masks that they're wearing, which are made of satin and
feathers, will be tossed to the blizzard at dawn.

ringer for an old lover, *who awaited me with cool drinks and a million flies.*

Trinculo, *of whom she's enamored,* is already saddled with a wife.

The green kimono, *which normally fell to his knees,* flapped flagrantly in the stirring heat.

The smoke, *which felt like sautéed silk,* sailed over us with no joy in our whereabouts.

The masks that they're wearing, *which are made of satin and feathers,* will be tossed to the blizzard at dawn.

Nola, *who came to the tea party in a pinafore,* was prepared for the riddles and white rats.

The lottery, *its first prize a wedding for two,* required blood tests and notes from the contestants' mothers.

ᴏᴈ❧ Phrases of all varieties generally go about with commas as sidekicks or confidants. An introductory participial or infinitive phrase also needs a comma unless it immediately precedes, and forms a part of, the subject or verb.

Entering the room, she found herself generously ignored.

Menacingly bopping down the road, the thug consulted his horoscope and decided to take the day off.

Ashamed to admit she'd been had by a shark, Marimba camouflaged her losses with a party on the *Santa Fanina* and a fanfare of loud new frocks.

Maimed and mangled from horsing around, we let Mucho Trabajo take us home.

Ululating through her tears and yanking her tresses,

the young widow paused to take a deep breath and admire herself in the mirror.

Stuffing her mouth with tarts, the duchess announced that she was leaving the country at the side of a worthless lout.

Aghast at this revelation, the duke backed into the fire and seriously singed his nether parts.

Ominously snuffling into her sleeve, the duchess departed into the black and inveigling night.

Tripping over the butler, she came into instant and all-around agonized focus through a circle of swiftly raised lorgnettes.

To get the rest of it off your chest, you would have to remove your shirt.

To remove the smudge from her record, she sorely effaced herself.

✧ Absolute phrases — phrases composed of a noun or pronoun plus a participle — that are not joined to the rest of

Skimming along the water was a cement truck full of mice.

the sentence by relationship words also need commas to set them off.

Her hands being cold, she plunged them into her inadequate pockets and tried to appreciate the snowstorm as an elemental treat.

Her hair matted with greasepaint and her magnificent torso protruding from a negligee of green nylon, she maundered through the apartment house next to her own, thrusting her key into each astounded door.

Formalities having been dispensed with, we got down to some low-class pizza.

He set out heartbrokenly for the receding border, there being no safety to count on in his homeland.

✧ A comma is used to set off a parenthetical clause, phrase, or word that is logically close to the rest of the sentence. Parenthetical elements less logically related to the rest of the sentence should be set off instead by dashes or parentheses.

The disconsolate child picked up the rubber remnants of his glorious red balloon and felt, in the flabby skin of such pathos, a darkness in the depths of his rubber soul.

Those spurs, I must say, are a provocative addition to your wardrobe.

Kristin Langfeldt — a regular bluestocking she was — held colloquies among the sybarites at her Saturday night at-homes.

The concert ended with a sonata (by then I was fast asleep) by Beethoven, Schumann, or Liszt.

*The hot flashes, although somewhat soothed by penguins
and ice cream, still startled her from sizzling slumbers,
scorched her sunsets with added intensity, and lit up
the dark side of her swoons.*

The hot flashes, although somewhat soothed by penguins and ice cream, still startled her from sizzling slumbers, scorched her sunsets with added intensity, and lit up the dark side of her swoons.

ᴑᴈ Some writers inadvertently—and incorrectly—insert a comma between a subject and its predicate. In the following sentences the comma should be deleted.

The letter she was writing, came to a clumsy close.

Our darling Timosha, expired last night after brushing your heart off his sleeve.

The chair she'd seen earlier in fluffy house slippers, wore patent leather shoes for affairs of state.

The beasts beyond the wilderness, have agreed to mate for life.

ᴑᴈ No comma separates the subject and predicate when their usual order is switched.

NOT: Of the utmost urgency on our agenda were, an interview with a raven, a rack of new nightgowns, a visit with our podiatrist, and a trip through the eyebrow of a hurricane in a boat with Wynken and Nod.

BUT: Of the utmost urgency on our agenda were an interview with a raven, a rack of new nightgowns, a visit with our podiatrist, and a trip through the eyebrow of a hurricane in a boat with Wynken and Nod.

ᴑᴈ A comma also should not get in the way of a verb and its object.

NOT: Odious flogged, our flagging spirits.

BUT: Odious flogged our flagging spirits.

NOT: We coughed up, some spare change and our handkerchiefs, but got away with our wasted lives.

BUT: We coughed up some spare change and our handkerchiefs, but got away with our wasted lives.

ↈ Use commas to set off the person or persons spoken to in direct address.

Come here, Nicolas, and hold my mouth shut with your big, spring-loaded hands.

Go right past the crockery, my dear, and then flash your way into the dark.

After you've washed your hands, ladies and gentlemen, you may sample our bonbons on your knees.

Alyosha, please tell me the rest of the story, with every lollygagger in place.

Friends, you needn't have come all this way just to have a tiff.

Darling, I'm in no condition for a protracted schmooze right now.

We'll have more than rhetorical and ontological questions, young lady, when we get to your whereabouts last night.

ↈ Appositives — words that follow a noun or pronoun and identify it — are usually set off by commas if they are nonrestrictive. Such words add parenthetical information.

Nobiscus Kahn, professor of angst, used to cry all over his lectern and ruin his lovingly prepared notes.

Charlotte Tingle, a sophomore, was the only girl at the lodge that night.

He lay dreaming of her little smile, a miracle of frailty and avarice.

Yolanta, the friend of detractors and sycophants alike, was waylaid by three brigands with fans.

Allegro non Troppo, the mastodons' kid brother, has trampled out his own bit of turf.

Her cat, Paw Beaucoup, knows how to give an admirable back rub with his well-tempered and discreet claws.

⌔ If she has other cats, with or without such talents — Gâteau, Toscanini, Desdemona, for example — we'd drop the comma setting off Paw Beaucoup's name, as it is now a restrictive appositive.

The poet Wallace Stevens was a pedestrian too.

James Joyce's novel *Ulysses* was once an article of coveted and contraband smut.

☞ If *Ulysses* were his only novel, and we couldn't also read his *Portrait of the Artist as a Young Man* and *Finnegans Wake*, the title *Ulysses* would be less essential to the meaning of the sentence, and therefore nonrestrictive.

⌔ When the appositive has become part of a proper name, the comma is omitted.

Eric the Red	Wilhelmina the Sad
Charles the Bold	Trixie the Perspicacious
Poco the Swift	Lambert the Fluffy

❧ Don't add commas to an already complex family situation: they're not needed before and after II, III, IV, etc., when used with full names handed down from one generation to the next. Juniors and Seniors, however, can go either way.

> Nimbus Torbach, Jr., has a glorious froth of clouds on his head like his dad's.
>
> Tropo Gallimauf III went off to seek his fortune in his granny's velvet vault.

❧ A comma is used between two adjectives when they modify the same noun and the word *and* can be inserted between them without altering the meaning.

> We entered a large, disreputable museum.
>
> He wanted to eat her peachy, creamy complexion with his souvenir spoon from Yellowstone Park.
>
> She let out a low, false chortle.
>
> She greeted him with open, entrenching arms.
>
> Time is a slippery, viscid, wavering tool of a malignant prestidigitator with nineteen thumbs.

❧ If the first adjective modifies the idea set forth by the second adjective and the noun combined, no comma is used between the adjectives.

> She lay tastefully dying in an unruffled green gown and never once complained.
>
> Her dull gold eyelids lifted heavily and fluttered one final coquettish farewell.
>
> Justinian gave a fond farewell pat to the long, sad face of his donkey.

❧ A comma follows the exclamatory *oh* but not the vocative *O*.

> Oh, how ridiculous!
>
> O gentle king . . .
>
> Oh, regrettable night!
>
> Oh, really now, kiddo!
>
> Oh, perilous thighs!
>
> Oh, perfidious lips!
>
> O Angel of Death . . .

❧ A comma is used to set off conjunctive adverbs, such as *however, moreover,* etc., and transitional adverbs.*

> We hate your ideas; however, we will give them proper consideration.
>
> What is love, after all, but a cross between two wishes?

❧ Use commas to set off interjections, however mild, transitional adverbs, and other expressions that cause a break in the flow of thought. Sometimes they begin a sentence; other times they balance it in the middle.

> Yes, we do toenails and teeth.
>
> No, you may not take a look at my tattoos.
>
> Well, she feels like some phenomenon, but she's really just a shaken belief.
>
> Dear me, how you have sacrificed your ethereal beauty for a life of greed and smut.

---

*See Semicolon chapter for a full spectrum of conjunctive adverbs.

Are you, perhaps, something less than sated?

Yes, it was a lamentably light meal.

Um, I would like another one, and in a different glass.

Sorry, we don't deal in ultimatums.

Yup, looks like we'll be needing some more leeches for those outrageous eyebrows.

Those mastodons, I do declare, must have gone to finishing school.

Well, well, what shall we boys think up next?

⌘ When such expressions don't break the continuity and no pause is needed, commas can be left out.

We are perhaps rather tedious company after some of the places you've been.

I do in fact prefer raucous company, but am delighted to be here nevertheless.

We did therefore have a pleasant evening of staring numbly amongst ourselves.

⌘ Two or more complementary or antithetical phrases referring to a single word that follows them should be set off from one another and from the following words by commas.

His delicate, though at the same time rough, cheek brushed against her sleeve and ripped it to silken shreds.

The most desired, if not the least convenient, seat in the house was taken by a dummy in diamonds and furs.

Your conclusions lead me away from, rather than toward, what you want me to think.

❧ An antithetical phrase or clause starting with *not* should be set off by commas if it is unessential to the meaning of the modified element.

He is a man of the world, not the punk you take him for.

The women in the room, not the men, are the best judges of the sexism of that remark.

I came to you, not to hear your stories, but to bounce upon your knee.

BUT —

I came to you not so much to hear your stories as to bounce upon your knee.

❧ Interdependent antithetical clauses should be set off by a comma.

The less she knew about the other woman, the more elaborate and tormenting her fantasies became.

Think what you wish, I'll never go dancing again.

The lower she sank, the better she felt.

❧ Short antithetical phrases, though, don't require commas.

The sooner the better.

The more the merrier.

I came to you not so much to hear your
stories as to bounce upon your knee.

THE SERIAL COMMA

✺ Three or more elements in a series are separated by commas. When the last two elements (words, phrases, or clauses) in a series are joined by a conjunction, a comma comes before the conjunction — unless you're a journalist.

Across her pellucid and guileless complexion danced a motley choir of alibis, innuendos, disguises, and sobriquets.

He looked at her face, her thighs, her hands for some sign of approbation, but everything about her was glancing away in the direction of something he could not name or escape.

We gave ourselves over to an interregnum of discord, mockery, and delight.

The rest of the story can be figured out by gossip, slander, and false report.

A great gnashing of teeth and popping of knuckles followed, many hard feelings got thwacked about, and many wings were bruised.

The oleaginous hors d'oeuvres were followed by beakers of vodka, remorse, and cold soup.

He is walking up walls, crawling sideways, and turning somersaults as he approaches the queen.

She attended the wedding feast in her Buster Brown collar, her water moccasins, her spring-loaded pelvic girdle, and her coiffeur's interpretation of Medusa at the Mardi Gras.

The turgid prose of the wedding ceremony gave way at the gala reception to biting remarks, caustic canapés, and drunken apologies, which the newly-weds fled in a rented BMW for a little spa frequented by clerics and crooks.

✣ When elements in a series are very simple and are all joined by conjunctions, no commas are used.

The truth of her checking account was mysterious and awkward and sad.

Blood and sweat and tears are all equally delectable to that renegade vampire.

He thought the remark she'd made was brilliant or irrelevant or mad.

She led a complicated and secret quotidian existence of matinees and intrigues and regrets.

Terror and beauty and flying fur were only the beginning of our revels that night.

Light of foot and dark of mind, she set off into the shrubbery with her needlepoint and a bunch of grapes and a basket of vipers and thread.

Once Alyosha and Jean-Pierre had slapped their mug shots onto their visas, they broke some plates and ate some blini and drank a toast to Chichikov.

✣ And now we have a serial comma in the company of a serial killer:

The Grim Reaper was cutting capers in the vestibule, attractively wagging his finger, and suggestively rolling his eyes. (This sultry gigolo knew the Straits of Gibraltar well: in a single night he had his way with both the Baba of Tangier and the Baba of Seville.)

In the intensity of her fervor to blend in with the decor, she tracks blood across the parlor rug, insults the hostess,* steps on the tail of the Great Dane sleeping peacefully before the roaring fire, and spatters the walls with oysters so reluctant to relinquish their shells.

⊃◈ When a series is concluded with *etc.* in the middle of a sentence, the *etc.* is set off by commas.

He told her he was into shuffleboard, soap operas, Lawrence Welk, etc., before she managed to slip out the back door.

She powdered her nose, her body, her alibis, etc., to meet his scrutiny intact.

⊃◈ A comma is used after terms such as *that is, i.e., e.g.,* and *namely* when they are used to introduce a series or an example.

Some of our members, namely, Alice, Bambi, and Bruno, had better watch out what they are saying these days.

After that we toured the hinterlands, specifically, Bosoxia, Azuriko, and Blegue.

---

*The hostess is wearing the Emerald Settee Skirt. Several ladies are nimbly seated upon her, balancing teacups, cookies, and kittens on their knees, as her untamed guest wreaks her ingenuous havoc throughout the room.

I advise you to split, i.e., beat it, get out, if you know what's good for you and your howling family.

✧ On occasion a comma must appear to prevent mistaken junction.

> To Lila, Nemo was ever a forethought.
>
> To Nemo, Lila was barely an afterthought.
>
> He followed her career as it rose and flowered, and applauded each new whiff of success she snorted on her distant but lonely laurels.
>
> Shortly after, the convocation commenced its pompous tones and hollow notes.

✧ Sometimes for easier reading two identical words or words close in sound or appearance should be separated by a comma.

> They came in, in striped pants and spats.
>
> Whatever happens, happens because it must.
>
> The time of need having passed, the time of having, having come . . .
>
> They went to sea, to see and be seen.

✧ Unrelated numbers are also separated by a comma.

> In 1905, 763 mustaches were shaved off in one county in Massachusetts alone.

✧ Although they are not necessary, commas may be used to set off a phrase indicating place of residence or origin directly after a person's name.

Mimi Mulash of Dobrocanto entered the hall with a pie.

Serving a pie to the seven ministers was Mimi Mulash, of Dobrocanto.

꩜ However, with historical figures whose places of residence or origin have become part of their names, the comma should be omitted.

Ivanka of Azuriko   Princess Beloved of Babylon
Eleanor of Aquitaine   Alexander of Macedonia
Ludwig of Bavaria   Annie of Ostria

꩜ Words identifying a person's title or position are set off from the person's name by commas. You may recognize this as a particular form of appositive.

Marina Kasnar, director of Ariadne auf SoHo, slipped out of the symposium on New Wave labyrinths at the Hotel Flambeau.

Sola Crespusci, poetry critic for *Licking the Beast,* was deluged with complimentary copies of the most aberrant works.

꩜ Commas are used to separate the parts of addresses and names of geographical places or political divisions.

Hotel Flambeau, 29 Hot Rod Parkway, Amplochacha, Blegue.

Nimbo Moostracht, Vice President, Eurobanque, 18 Rue des Ecouffes, 75004, Paris, France.

I flew my horse from Morski, Louvelandia, to Southpaw, Califonica, in five nights of shooting stars.

*I flew my horse from Morski, Louvelandia, to Southpaw,
Califonica, in five nights of shooting stars.*

❧ In dates, the comma between month and year is optional, but commas must set off the year whenever it immediately follows the day.

> In January 1979 a host of angels was espied off the shores of Lake Bled in a pleasure boat emanating the black and blues notes of early jazz.

> I was born on March 17, 1947, on a cold bed of river sand.

> On 31 October 1972 a gang of hoodlums disguised as mendicant children gained entrance to the doomed château.

> She came out of the forest on May 7, 1956, to take her place among her fellow femmes fatales.

❧ A comma is used to indicate omitted words readily understood from the context.

> The farmer takes a wife; the wife, a child; the child, a dog; the dog, another child; the other child, another dog; the other dog, a pet rabbit to chase.

> Jean-Pierre splutters with dirty raindrops; Mr. Thundermum, with moral indignation.

> Nola was a striking strawberry blonde; Angela, a startled brunette.

> Heidi took out her Swiss army knife; Gabriel, his tuning fork.

> Nimbus drank hemlock; Jean-Pierre, Perrier.

❧ A comma follows the complimentary close of letters.

Yours unflappably,
 Jespera Trost

A rain of kisses upon your wife and children,
 Jonquil Mapp

As always, and
 then some,
 Blaze Cinders

With all the sincerity I can muster,
 Hugo Z. Scott

⊃⟡ A comma comes between every third digit, counting
 from the right, in numbers of one thousand and over.

196,950,000 miles to Loona's uncle's

564,000 ways to keep company

⊃⟡ Commas separate inverted names, phrases, etc., as in a
 bibliography, index, or catalogue.

Codrescu, Andrei
Ivanjicki, Olja
Kirkenlied, Stella
Owen, Seena
Sachs, Harvey
Swift, Savannah

Buckle, H. T., 20
Buddha, 82
Buffon, 214
Bukharin, *see* Buxarin, Ni-
 kolaj Ivanovič
Buxarin, Nikolaj Ivanovič,
 27, 168, 169-170, 184, 239

"Corrugated Pantaloons"
Garden of Burning Bridges, The
Girl with the Golden Eyesore, The
Gossamer and the Green Light
"Handful of Mist"
"Metamorphosis, The"
"Trombone of Parma, The"

🗝 A comma follows the salutation of a personal letter.

> Dear Rosie and Nimrod,
>   Thank you for the hospitality, the cold bath water, the stale beer, and everything.
> Dear Nimbo,
>   You make me talk big in my sleep.

🗝 A quotation, maxim, proverb, or similar expression should be set off from the rest of the sentence by commas.

> "I've been wondering, Jasmine," said Jimmy shyly, "if you'd care to sit out this tango in my lap."
> As he usually did when entering a strange room or arrangement, he thought fondly and desperately of his motto, "Be cool," which never did him any good.

🗝 If the quotation is the subject, predicate nominative, or restrictive appositive of the sentence, the comma should not be used.

> "Get out, and take your mucus with you" was hardly the sympathetic greeting the flu victim expected from his healthy friends.

You're the cat's meow, no?

"I wanna lick the syrup off your hotcakes" was her favorite line in a song by Jusko Bou.

❧ A comma comes before a confirmatory—or confirmation-seeking—question always and only when the main clause is declarative and the second part is interrogative.

You'd like some more clafouti, right?

They're suspects in the Appenzeller heist, aren't they?

She's a runaway from Louvelandia, isn't she?

You're the cat's meow, no?

❧ A comma is not used with an indirect quote.

G. K. Chesterton says that coincidences are spiritual puns.

Sola Crespusci remarked to her cohorts that poetry is mostly vacant exercises done at majestic hours, and resigned from her thankless job.

❧ A comma should not be used to set off a quotation that flows into the rest of the sentence.

He responded with a hallucinated "I see."

Stella Kirkenlied described disappointment as "a flattened-out anticipation" that is "rarely a prelude to something worse."

Hal Kanter, who had spent several days with Elvis, wrote of a young man with "ancient eyes" and a "child's mouth" who "awoke from the nightmare of poverty to find the brilliant sun of Fame suddenly burst in his eyes."

He responded with a hallucinated "I see."

✳ When a comma is called for at the end of material within quotation marks, parentheses, or brackets, it goes inside the quotation marks but outside the parentheses or brackets.

For Max Ernst, collage was "an exploration of the fortuitous encounter upon a nonsuitable plane of two mutually distant realities," and that definition is still relevant today.

Sola Crespusci, defining photography as "light plus the impulse to see more than it can reveal," took to photographing slices of the unexpected in the wondrous back alleys of chance.

She scrunched her shoulder up next to his (all the while thinking of Timofey), and the shadows obligingly obliterated what was wrong with his face.

We were not thunderstruck (not even stunned), and her disappointing announcement gave way to a game of cards.

The

Semicolon

YOUR WRITING—anybody's—doesn't clamor for semi-colons among all its marks with words. Most of the time commas and periods will take care of linking and separating in the midst of sentences and between them. Semicolons, un-like commas, are for separating only, when a period is a tougher break than what your sense demands.

A semicolon comes between closely related independent clauses that are not linked by a coordinating conjunc-tion. Extended clauses that contain commas certainly need a semicolon if a period is not wanted, but brief in-dependent clauses might also be most appropriately sep-arated with the soft pause this symbol holds.

> Oh, I often click my tongue; it's my only revenge.
>
> Sit down; I'll make us some coffee and some suspirations.
>
> At one time this land was roamed by buffalo and free ponies; today it is rare to see either on a day's journey through wilderness or town.

Nadia was halted and removed in a squad car; they charged her with lurking with intent to loiter, and with wearing someone else's heart up her sleeve.

I'm very ocular in my reading habits; take *away* your books on cassettes!

Anjula was despondent; she'd come in the wrong shoes.

That incorrigible sensualist, Samuel Johnson, wrapped in a peignoir and a mild euphoria and at work on his dictionary, bounces little words up and down on one knee; Scheherazade sits on the other knee, smoking Turkish cigarettes and interrupting his noble labors with her own retellings of classic children's tales.

❧ The semicolon shows itself to great advantage through the balance or contrast it offers between two or more similarly constructed clauses.

> The tower was too high; the dungeon was too low.
>
> A flannel nightgown is transfixed by a religious experience; a silk slip has a close call.
>
> Days are in disorder; nights clump around the bar.
>
> The little maestro slept fitfully; the cellist practiced relentlessly; the house pets conversed softly with the maid.
>
> One flustered voter considers the candidate's voice raspy; another calls it twangy.

❧ A semicolon punctuates the elements in a series for which a clearer division than that provided by commas is needed — or if too many commas confuse.

> The contestants for the breakfast-eating championship came from Lompoc, Rhode Island; Laundro, Green Hungary; Gravona, New Shropshire; and other places we'd never heard of.
>
> Attending the kickoff of the global warming conference were a paranormal guttersnipe from Trinity College; seven Volga boatmen singing "The Song of the Volga Boatmen"; an extraterrestrial water sprite and his girlfriend from Tulsa, Oklahoma; a hypochondriac with his ice packs and hot-water bottle; and a ferry-boater, in a tux, from the river Styx.

❧ When the following conjunctive adverbs are used transitionally between clauses of a compound sentence, they should be preceded by a semicolon: *accordingly, afterward,*

The little maestro slept fitfully; the cellist practiced relentlessly;
the house pets conversed softly with the maid.

also, besides, consequently, earlier, furthermore, hence, however, indeed, later, likewise, moreover, naturally, nevertheless, nonetheless, otherwise, similarly, still, then, therefore, and *thus.*

We took one look at the first kitten and named her Cannelle (cinnamon); naturally, in no time at all, we were stroking the second one and calling her Flanelle (flannel).

There is always room for improvement; moreover, in this case that's all the room there is.

Samantha had had her fill of his blustering histrionics; thus, she spun on her heel and retreated to the coolness of her dimly lit boudoir.

We like the look of your face; however, we suspect that a troubled childhood is hidden by that beard.

⸎ Dangling from the wings of cherubim are numerous transitional or explanatory expressions that ask for treatment similar to that accorded conjunctive adverbs; they too are preceded by a semicolon when they link two independent clauses. Here is a sampling of this motley connecting collection:

after all	in addition	in any event
at length	at the same time	for this purpose
e.g.	in fact	in real terms
for example	on the contrary	in the meantime
i.e.	to be sure	on the other hand
for instance	viz.	equally important

We will do our utmost to make it festive; in any event, we'll have ice cream and hopscotch for the children, and babas au rhum and rumbas for their babas.

I don't have to let you walk all over me; after all, I have a mouth through which to negotiate, and a lexicon that has inspired many to precipitately take to their heels.

I've shown plenty of courage before; for instance, when the other ushers were quaking in their boots, I stepped right up to that bedizened chatelaine and put her soundlessly in her place.

That's a very interesting story; what's more, twenty percent of it at the very least may be partly true.

An insistent voice was braying on in the boxcar; in fact, it was inciting revolt against the drug lords of our fair Azurico.

ɔ⚜ A semicolon may be used between long clauses of a compound sentence, between clauses subdivided by commas, even between clauses with a conjunction joining them.

Jacob, who was sitting on the balcony watching her out of the corner of his steel-gray eye, lunged forward to touch her as she passed by; but someone grabbed a fistful of his collar from behind and said, "Lay off my woman, you jerk."

ɔ⚜ Semicolons separate items in bibliographic or footnote references, and behave similarly in less scholarly listings like radio program guides when other marks have been exhausted.

Haslam, Gerald, *That Constant Coyote* (1990); Mapp, Jonquil, *Glass Backwards* (1972); Nordan, Lewis, *Music of the Swamp* (1991).

Clementi: Sonata Quasi-Concerto in C, Op. 33, No.
    3; Dvořák: Serenade for Strings in E, Op. 22

Sibelius: Quartet in E-flat; Sibelius Academy
    Quartet.

꙳ The semicolon goes outside quotation marks and parentheses. When the parenthetical words explain something coming before, the semicolon follows the parentheses. When quoted matter ends with a semicolon, the
semicolon is dropped.

> He called her "The Little Prince"; she too had fallen
> to earth with a rose and golden curls.

> Yolanta seemed to think that everyone in the world
> had read "Rameau's Nephew Meets Rappacini's
> Daughter"; she referred to it in every conversation
> she had.

> This was only one of the signs of her coming dementia
> (many more were yet to manifest themselves); her
> delusions became progressively more literary and
> bizarre.

> We were outlining the program for the next three
> months (it was to include many visits to a rollicking
> taverna); objections came bumping in from the
> somber side of the room.

> Not only were we naked, crazed, and starving (and
> far from our warm little homes); we were without any
> good books as well.

The
Colon

❧

THERE'S SOMETHING assertively expectant about a colon: setting up both the reader and the sentence, it would be heartless and unfaithful to let either one down. This is what I mean: what follows the colon further explains, illustrates, or restates, with precise, embellished, or loquacious variation, the words leading up to the colon. This is so often the case that if the goods are not delivered, you deserve to feel betrayed: *forthcoming* is the colon's middle name. Our cover girl, Loona, who winds up in the Brackets chapter with a colon bridging the gap between her actions and her words, could be a zombied mannequin for this mark: see how her lissome weight is poised on tiptoes in a vigil of pacing and pausing until the anticipated arrival suddenly becomes a thing of the past. But these snake eyes shouldn't keep you waiting: gratification is immediate.

:   :   :   :

ɔ❧ A colon is used to introduce a part of a sentence that exemplifies, restates, or explains the preceding part.

Some of the world's great monsters have untold stories: many, in fact, lead quite happy childhoods before
their later, more infamous years.

I've led a sheltered life: I've gone from one shelter to
another.

Pain stood in the way like a sheet of glass: you could
walk through it, but not without a certain noise.

The effect *was* striking: snuffling furry beasts and bald-

*Some of the world's great monsters have untold stories: many, in
fact, lead quite happy childhoods before their
later, more infamous years.*

headed women singing *a cappella* on a lifeboat solemnly trawling the flooded corridors of the Capitol.

This is how I found him: mesomorphic, monosyllabic, and debonair.

⊃◈ In the same vein, the colon as annunciation:

Next on the runway came Gregor Schlaffenfuss's Wombat Fatigues: pockets and cuffs edged in wombat fur, and beaming and riveted with sleepy wombat eyes.

I'll level with you straightaway, Toots: I *was* standing by your man while you were off renovating the camper.

⊃◈ Elaboration or elucidation:

Out-of-town parents and merchandise from Colombia: a recipe for compromised youth.

Zoombach's transvestite *Hamlet* was a total flop: it left both the critics and its opening night audience uncomprehendingly and unsympathetically stunned.

⊃◈ It is thus that a colon points out an important appositive:

Besides sniffing cigars and snapping suspenders, there was one thing sure to be on the tycoons' agenda: money.

One expedition that promises high spirits must not be entered into lightly: the one to the wine and olives of that taverna after many bumpy switchback curves.

✺ The colon is used to introduce a series or list.

> The pajamas she so implacably desired came in a tantalizing spectrum of allusive colors: I Am Epicurious Yellow; By the Light of My Mooncalf; and Chacun à Son Blue.

> Such are the blessings of which I am fully aware: (1) a mother with wild young hormones; (2) a pasture with satyrs and centaurs; (3) a view of the roving heavens from my trundle bed.

> These are the reasons for his absenteeism: fear of furniture; aversion to numbers and dollar signs; a snakebite on his chin.

> Coco concentrated her study on three twentieth-century French writers: Raymond Queneau, Blaise Cendrars, and Max Jacob.

✺ If the list or series comes after an expression such as *namely, for instance, for example,* or *that is,* a colon should be used only if the series consists of one or more grammatically complete clauses.

> Coco's study was concentrated on three twentieth-century French writers, namely, Queneau, Cendrars, and Max Jacob.

> For example: Queneau is the author of *The Bark Tree;* Cendrars wrote *To the End of the World;* and Jacob confected epiphanies into household words and streetwise scenes.

✺ A colon is not necessary or welcome if an incomplete statement precedes the list (e.g., a verb without a complement, a preposition without an object, etc.).

Jean-Pierre's pals on the tower were Josiane, Pauline, and Chosette.

The teething rats are especially fond of Romano, Asiago, and Mimolette.

BUT: The baby vampire tries out his baby teeth on surfaces that are fun to puncture: golf balls, plastic Coke bottles, balloons.

ꙮ The terms *as follows* and *the following* require a colon if followed immediately by the illustrating or listed items or if the introducing clause is incomplete without such items.

The way to her heart was as follows: take a left many times and then go straight.

The following people will be shipped a dozen yellow roses upon their respective demises: Chortle T. Ash-bottom, Percy Q. Festivall, Dorothy Lambleton, and Nestor Craymom.

Doomed, a roman à clef, contains the following characters: Heidi, Horvath, Gabriel, Angela, and the Spanish lady from Spain.

ꙮ If the introducing statement is complete and is followed by complete sentences, a period may be used instead.

A guide to the churches follows. Each one is to be visited in its turn. The village is full of them.

1. Begin with the Metropolitan Church of the Art of Jesus the Conductor . . .

ꙮ A colon is used to introduce an extended quotation.

The speaker rose, shuffled his feet, and spoke: "It wasn't always that people wore red shoes . . ."

Loona's letter to Rosie and Nimrod continues: "I was left with the many invisible things that crawl over my body the night after the night you were two of them."

The advice of a dying Roman father to his sons: "My sons, you must all try to have an occupation in life. Life without an occupation is contemptible and meaningless. But always remember this: you must never allow your occupation to degenerate into work."
— Luigi Barzini, *The Italians*

A colon comes between the chapter and verse numbers in biblical references.

Noah's long, wet story begins in Genesis 5:28.

᎓❦ A colon is used between the volume and page numbers in references to multivolume works and periodicals.

> We got a rundown on gazelles in the *Encyclopedia Laconia* 8:147.

᎓❦ A colon appears after the salutation of a business letter.

> Dear Sir:
> I wish to complain, without seeming to, for otherwise I am completely satisfied with all your errors, ineptitude, and faux pas.
>
> Dear Mr. Gallimauf:
> Enclosed are the bonbon samples we have seen fit to bombard you with in our first attack on your pocketbook and family name . . .

᎓❦ Personal letters, you will rejoice, follow the salutation with a curvaceous comma:

> My darling Jacaranda,

We got a rundown on gazelles in the
Encyclopedia Laconica *8:147.*

❧ In another aspect of correspondence, a colon is used between the initials of the dictator of a letter and its typist:

KS:cd

❧ A colon separates hours from minutes in expressions of time.

The man in the red cape followed me until 2:17, when he was seen stepping into the men's john for a change of clothes, a new profession, or a change of scene.

❧ A colon may separate a heading from the material it describes or introduces.

An accomplished man: no trouble with strange fastenings

Falling in love: I was acting in accord with my favorite hyperboles.

HELP WANTED: Retired, active couple to menace small mobile-home park.

Headline: STREET HUSTLERS EVADE SCHEHERAZADE

Sign on librarian's desk: REVENGE

A drug: It gives you back all the headaches the world has stolen from you.

Pleasantry: a privileged, pampered social class

Disappointment: a flattened-out anticipation

Wanted: brisk young ballerina with Italian and feather duster for conversation and light housekeeping.

A valentine: Oh, to be up against you.

Obituary: TWO DECLARED DEAD IN TINY SOB.

❧ A colon separates the name of a character from his or her lines in a play.

> LADY ZIPWORTH: All I do is wait for your clumsy hands to make mincemeat of my apparel.

❧ A colon is used to separate the title and subtitle of a book.

> *The Mourning of the Logicians: A History of the Decline of Reason in Western Civilization*
> *Om, Om on the Range: Cowboys and Meditation*
> *Lipstick Traces: A Secret History of the Twentieth Century*
> *Dead Elvis: A Chronicle of a Cultural Obsession*
> *Intimate Apparel: A Dictionary of the Senses*

❧ The colon should appear outside quotation marks or parentheses. When material ending with a colon is quoted, the colon is dropped.

> There was one thing that left her unsatisfied at the end of that novella (*The Telltale Toothbrush*): she never found out who the heroine really was.

> She winced at his response of such a gratuitous "Wow": it said little for his seizure of her meaning and even less for his lexicon.

> He had a strenuous objection to the poem "Suddenly What Sings in Me Dies of Boredom": it was a blatant piece of plagiary.

Wanted: brisk young ballerina with Italian and feather duster
for conversation and light housekeeping.

The

Hyphen

❧

I WON'T EVEN attempt to downplay my preference for one of the hyphen's most engaging, hot properties: its capacity to create new words and open up new meanings through combinations both established and original. This procreation is so much a normal part of verbal life that such coinages often go through stages: initially two words stand separately, eyeing each other, but already making a move toward a brave new union. The next phase finds the two holding hands through the go-between, our obliging hyphen. Eventually they run into each other's arms and seamlessly begin a new life asoneword. Lots of words were formed this way. We blink without before-and-after seeing, until we accidentally drop and break one of these clasping couplets, and the shattered pieces speak to us of how they once ran free.

❧ A hyphen connects the parts of some compound words used as nouns or adjectives. It is also used in some words formed with prefixes.

Let's turn on the posttrauma make-believe.

He pounded upon her ill-tempered clavicles with a bacchanalian bravado that calmed his seething soul.

The starry-eyed sycophant prowled about the antechamber in her underwear, her catlike movements foreshadowing the self-conscious grace of the imminent and all-out attack.

"That was a curiosity-provoking peepshow," said the pseudosophisticated ball of fire to the pink-faced stick-in-the-mud as they cuddled halfheartedly over a pint of bitter in a neo-Gothic hole-in-the-wall.

A well-known cross-eyed scholar-poet with gray-blue eyes and coal-black hair drove many an ill-favored maiden to madness with his devil-may-care attitude and his Sturm-und-Drang panache.

❧ But a hyphen is not used when a compound adjective or other modifier follows the noun.

His off-color bagpipes are seriously out of tune.

His out-of-tune bagpipes have been hidden in my room.

He was a door-to-door salesman of housewares and eyesores.

He sold housewares and eyesores door to door.

❧ When a compound begins with an adverb ending in -ly, a hyphen is out of the question.

a freakishly attired ombudsman

that profoundly regretful ratcatcher

an insanely coiffed concubine

her recently slimmed haunches

her neatly categorized notions of human frailty

⊃✤ Herewith a scattered spectrum of merged and hyphen-ated and not nearly touching compound words:

a no-win situation   painkiller

archfiend

star-crossed   ·   bankroll

razzmatazz

artsy-craftsy

prefabricated false pretenses

string quartet

credit card

amateur night   night light

shoe store   walking papers

In *The Winter's Tale* we find "a snapper-up of uncon-sidered trifles."

Well, I'm off to the shoe store to see if my walking pa-pers are ready.

⊃✤ If you're compounding your own perceptions into new words, their meaning and genesis will be more apparent if the happy issue is hyphenated. My own example, prompted by a betrayal: I was lurch-left by his abnega-tion. A knuckle-rapping, squint-eyed editor reprimand-ed me when I wrote of "jet-lagging around Europe and the South Pacific," when it seemed to me (and still does) a perfectly natural offspring, since we lag and are lag-ging all the time, with no hope of ever catching up and with no airplanes in sight.

Since it is year-round mating season and mad tea party all at once in this territory, I gladly abandon at-tempts to enlighten on the rules and their exceptions among compounded and compounding words. The dictionary is useful if a magnifying glass is at hand: the bold black dots used to indicate syllable breaks so closely mimic the hyphens of sharper breaks that you'll be cross-eyed before being reassured.

These are among my many reasons for not codifying the compound phenomenon, and for jumping into the party without further trepidation, taking you with me, I hope.

They broke the story with such extra-extra-read-all-about-it verisimilitude that neither the victors nor the victims could figure out how to raise objections to its manifold lies.

This is a quality-of-life issue, not a Moral-Majority-lack-of-perspective dead horse.

Over the river floated a moon-stroked maiden with flowers and all the frills in her sails.

her down-to-earth feet and large, airborne voice

a shaped-up shut-in living happily inside her skin, at cross-purposes with sin and gin

catwalk   carryover

      thunderstorm

                       quiet sun

            ribbon lightning

    an uncalled-for crack

                 a meanspirited comeback

      an off-the-cufflinks interview

                   sugar-coated

     user-ingratiating

           bald-headed Sally

In German, words formed by combining other words which then appear without hyphens are a common sight. They don't stop with two: these concoctions can include four or five words all joining in to create one new specific meaning. French is more discreet about such indiscriminate comminglings, but a coupling is often to be seen, sometimes a real beauty:

kite is *cerf-volant,* or flying deer

bat is *chauve-souris,* or bald mouse

Some of us tumble into hyphenated first names or surnames at birth. Others create such surnames, in marriage, for example, joining one name with another. Hyphenated surnames are usually considered as one word.

Too-Too LaBlanca

Jean-Jacques Passera

Suzanne Benton-Bria

Laurinda Travers-Moostracht

Daniel Day-Lewis, by turns Romeo, pompadoured gay punk, Czech womanizer, albino Dracula, turn-of-the-century twit, itinerant dentist, Russian child-man poet, peripatetic watercolorist, and left-footed wonder, is my idea of a real man.

Proper names are not generally hyphenated when used as adjectives, but some proper names are always used as adjectives, and so require a hyphen:

African-American   Bosnian-Herzegovinian
Greco-Roman   Austro-Hungarian
Anglo-Saxon   Drogo-Amplochachan
Ludo-Rastislavan

❧ A hyphen expresses hesitation or stuttering.

"I'm d-d-delighted to see you again," she stammered, barring his way into the room with her big toe spread out to its full size.

❧ A hyphen indicates the spelling out of words.

"You are my darling, my d-a-r-l-i-n-g," said the spelling master to his rapt and evasive pupil as he opened her eyes to a whole new lexicon of shame.

❧ A hyphen shows syllabification—the break between syllables—at the end of a line.

When Jespera was depressed, and that was pretty often, she'd pluck her eyebrows and drink Southern Comfort and sing the most disgusting songs.

The impresario, declaring Gabor a lethal combination of talent and trouble, ripped up their itinerary for the new world order and suggested a year off with penguins and the song of the earth.

❧ Hyphens are also used to divide words into syllables for purposes of explication or pronunciation.

My name is Wilhelmina Trisolokian,
Wil-hel-min-a Tris-o-lo-ki-an.

❧ Hyphens help locate places, and not only in English.

Henley-on-Thames   St.-Germain-en-Laye
Swim-Two-Birds   Annandale-on-Hudson

*Over the river floated a moon-stroked maiden with flowers
and all the frills in her sails.*

❧ A hyphen joins compound numbers from twenty-one to ninety-nine and is used to express fractions.

> thirty-six
> eighty-seventh
> two-thirds

❧ But a fraction should not be hyphenated if one of its elements is already hyphenated.

> forty-four hundredths
> one sixty-fourth

❧ When numbers are not spelled out, hyphens link them with units of measurement to form adjectives. Money figures, however, are hyphenated only when spelled out.

> The 5,000-year-old fossil lay grinning in his palm.
> Their rendezvous at the Last Judgment Pinball Machine Motel turned into a 254-hour marathon that neither Torquil nor Jonquil would ever regret.
> A $5 million deficit smacks of the good old days.
> BUT—
> The waiter sniffed at his five-dollar tip and softly clucked his insouciant thanks.

❧ Hyphens are used to join numbers with other words:

> two-, three-, and four-room apartments
> seven-year itch
> ten-o'clock shadow
> fifth-form students
> a three-year tantrum

That poor child had a nine-month marination in her mother's margaritas.

The fifth-graders were channeled into the garden, their firecrackers surrendered at the gate.

ɔ❖ In the course of a normal sentence, spell out ages given.

Timofey would have been fifty-six had he lived to see this day.

Timofey is a forty-five-year-old corpse and an eleven-year-old ghost.

Nadia became his girlfriend when she was an eighteen-year-old rebel with painted claws.

Cannelle and Flanelle will be sixty-five days old tomorrow.

The
Dash

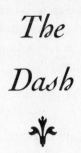

DASHES ARE OF two kinds, and one of them is further multiplied.

The en dash (the width of a capital *N*) leads a straight-laced life in schedules, bibliographies, timetables, which we'll get to later. The em dash (the width of a capital *M*) is much too energetic and impetuous to have its story put on hold: a streak, a comet flash, a leap across a gap, it's the most available of punctuation marks, just because its form and function sometimes seem the closest to the way we think and perceive relationships. It's really a sort of general factotum leapfrogger, turning reading, if it's overused, into acrobatics, and ousting commas, semicolons, colons, and parentheses from their rightful places. Use it effectively, and affectionately, but don't let it take over and become a stylistic tic.

Somewhat like a colon, but looking a bit more sudden and casual, an em dash can lead you to an upshot, a final summary word or statement, an abrupt appositive, and similarly can emphasize a particular word. This dash has a slight space or no space before and after, and computers have rescued it from being made, as on a typewriter, with two hyphens.

> He had one favorite maxim for the great white hunters — "Get lost."

> Sopranos, pianists, small boys carrying kittens on stage — none was spared her vituperative disdain.

> What — give up cringing?

> I'm not exactly leaving — I'm just spreading my tentacles.

> Were you reckless, shattered, or impervious in your forties — or none of the above?

> Sell your story to the tabloids: the sordid, the glamorous, the extraterrestrial — they'll love it.

> "Some of your fans will be there."
> "Oh, good — I'll wear my fan belt."
> — "The Mauled Scribe"

✺ The dash shows a break in continuity or thought in a sentence.

> Last night, as we slept together for the last time — where were you, anyway?

> I've had a lot of things on my mind lately — now what was I saying? — I mean, I can't concentrate, cogitate, ruminate; why are you looking at me that way?

✺ A dash sets off parenthetical material that results from or creates a break in thought or continuity.

I cleaned my sealskin — and what a chore it was! — only to find that there were fifty more filthy ones beneath it waiting for the same treatment from me.

It was twilight — if there ever was a time to match that word — and the bats were flitting in and out of the pergola.

Charmiane left us for a moment to lock her drawer — God only knows what she keeps in there! — and fetch her opera glasses and cigars.

∋✦ The dash is used to emphasize an appositive.

More than just a book — it's a major piece of torture.

Theodora, my beloved — my only soporific — how sweet of you to tuck me into bed.

I have this small scale of torment to play — a cacophony of everything that could possibly go wrong.

The Grim Reaper — that cosmopolitan gadabout — was cutting capers in the vestibule while a daffy dowager quaffed her Darjeeling and knocked back vermouth and schnapps.

Mardi Gras — Fat Tuesday — has its hottest time in Rio.

∋✦ A pair of dashes is used to enclose words for an abrupt emphasis or other stylistic effect. Appositional phrases may also be shown off in this way.

They gave — let there be no doubt about it — a thunderous ovation.

Miranda — her T-shirt still splattered with blood — tucked her incorrigible friend under her wing and led her off, tendering apologies to the astounded hostess, guests, and Great Dane, whose whimpers were unbecoming to a beast of his stature.

Through an emissary no one would ever suspect of *this* affiliation — a Mozart maniac in a red cape — the consortium brought their competitors to their knees so they could ply them with bonbons.

The rats under suspicion — the ones whose tails we're on, that is — got away in a stolen truck as its driver was making a delivery to a *fromagerie* in the Rue du Dragon.

She has the most delightful way of greeting you over the telephone — as if she's fluttering her nose and recalling some innocent indiscretion you'd committed recently that you wish had gone unnoticed — and yet the intimacy of this wordless allusion makes you want to talk your heart out to her and no one else far into the night.

I have no doubt whatsoever that there still lives in me someone powerful, a kind of athlete — or rather the wreckage of an athlete — a torso without arms or legs, who painfully moves within my body thereby tormenting both himself and me.

— Yury Olesha,
No Day Without a Line

Fed up with all this coy nomenclature, she insisted he cease referring to his new flame as The Little Prince and call her Bambi, Jacaranda — or whatever her name was — instead.

Charmiane left us for a moment to lock her drawer — God only
knows what she keeps in there! — and fetch
her opera glasses and cigars.

✎ Punctuation before a dash is ordinarily eliminated. When words enclosed by a dash call for a question mark or exclamation point, it precedes the dash. When punctuation is intrinsic to the meaning of the dashed material, include it.

> My uncle Nimbo — he's a big Eurobanker; did I tell you? — just amplified my dowry with the sorts of trinkets that would go over big in Azuriko — a land of landed gentry and lapis lakes and rivers rushing in to steal the meadows.

> You *did* say — or was I ascribing to you emotions you did not in fact feel? — that you thought of me all the way to Pontito.

> Officials of the international — not interspecies — beauty teen princess pageant accepted the lovely lamia without knowing who — or what — she was.

☞ If dashed material brings you to the end of a sentence, the dash disappears and the sentence ends with whatever punctuation mark is appropriate.

✎ A dash is used before the citation or source of a quotation.

> "I hear as the stags in the underwood hear when they raise, point, and lower the great hairy auricles of their independent pink ears." — Henri Michaux

> "Unrequited love's a bore." — Billie Holiday

> "The book you mention, I have not met. Thank you for tenderness." — Emily Dickinson

> "One cannot create without a little sluttishness packed away somewhere." — Rebecca West

❧ An en dash indicates journeys when one or both of the origin and destination adjectives are compound or hyphenated.

San Sebastian–Ljubljana flight

La Rochelle–Paris train

Amorgas–St. Hippolyte express

Vancouver–Bowen Island ferry

Baton Rouge–New Orleans bus

He left on the Nismer–East Blagundia express in haste and in hopes of having a good lunch.

❧ An en dash generally likes to team up with numbers in all their usual places: continuing or inclusive times, dates, page numbers, and paragraph citations.

1048–50

1914–1984

pp. 1072–1138

article 4, section 8, paragraphs 3.11–3.85

Gradimir the Timid lived 1439–1502.

You will find the secret of the lost Albanian on pages 89–111.

The abbreviated hours for the new city library are Tuesday–Thursday, 12–4, and that is all.

The Lobelia Relocation Office is open 1:00–4:30 daily and would be glad to relocate your lobelias, or anything else you want misplaced.

❧ To indicate a time span in the future, a conjecture, fantasy, conservative estimate, prognosis for or against longevity, etc., an en dash will represent them all.

*... just amplified my dowry with the sorts of trinkets that would
go over big in Azuriko — a land of landed gentry and lapis
lakes and rivers rushing in to steal the meadows.*

the Clinton presidency (1993–)

Lada Larkovich (1982–)

☞ As you may notice on these pages and on other surfaces that have rejoiced in your reading of them, no spacing is wanted or needed before or after this dash. It sticks closely to its figures, words, and letters.

✤ While we're in this techno-corner, I should add that on a computer, with its own little en dash at the flick of two fingers, or some similar gesture, this mark is used like a hyphen, or instead of it, to show halting or hesitant speech.

"Y–y–you took away my t–t–toy t–t–t–truck!"

✤ A 2-em dash steps in for missing letters in a word, whether it's discretion, censorship, ignorance, or impatience that brought this blankness on.

O——ti (Onetti?)

J——Other

That f——ing troglodyte!

✤ This description from *Intimate Apparel* willfully shows how liberal use of the dash is distracting and obfuscates relationships.

That incorrigible sensualist, Samuel Johnson, wrapped in a peignoir and a mild euphoria and at work on his dictionary, bounces little words up and down on one knee. Scheherazade sits on the other knee, smoking Turkish cigarettes and interrupting his noble labors with her own intimate versions of Hans Christian Andersen tales and the brothers Grimm,

• 93 •

and lots of other stories from who knows where —
perhaps from the body of a muslin dummy whose
ripped kneecap has spilled shredded manuscripts into
a Croatian seamstress's hands on a Caribbean
cruise — things like *Don Juan Is a Woman* and *The Un-
finished Cookie* — while Boswell cuts capers about the
room or groans on the sofa over the condition he's
been left in by his latest debaucheries.

✺ A 3-em dash with a space on each side indicates an omitted or missing word. In bibliographies, this long dash
spares us the repetition of an author's name.

Your acupuncturist will be expecting you at ——
Monday, May 10.

Babar is the king of —— in his red suit and patent
leather shoes.

Bantock, Nick. *Griffin and Sabine.* Chronicle Books,
San Francisco, 1991.
——. *The Egyptian Jukebox.* . . .
——. *The Golden Mean.* . . .

Quotation
Marks

><✦ Quotation marks enclose direct quotations and dialogue.

"I gather," said Rosie, "that you've made up your mind in an unmade bed."

"Gosh, the moon looks just like something from outer space," breathed Heidi in cosmic awe.

She said, "As a rule I hate iguanas, but this one had a wistful face."

The tampon ad read: "First she was a woman — then she was a teenager."

"Are you a nurse?"
"Yes, I'm nursing vipers in my bosom."

"I will make myself black trousers of the velvet of my voice." — Vladimir Mayakovsky

"Shadows delightfully crossed the tearinches of a headache." — Boris Lopatin

"These crawdads are downright petrified," growled Grandpa, shaking a fist at the microwave.

"Which is the hand to kiss?"

"The hand to kiss is the one you've frightened away."

"What are tears, anyway," she sobbed in his arms, "but little refugees from the ocean?"

Quentin Crisp elucidated, "No one wants to get into his grave still feeling frisky."

"And you can still smile after all those broken bottles and all that bad press?" he asked.

"Are you a student?"

"No, I'm a visiting metaphysician."

"Belated kisses must be unpacked."
— Boris Lopatin, *The Surreal Suitcase*

"Do you want me to rub your back?"

"I want you to back into my rubble."

✺ For dialogue, begin a new paragraph for each change of speaker.

"Why, she's nothing but a retired flowerpot!" declared Gregor Schlaffenfuss.

"That's the cruelest remark I've heard since I was a gawky debutante," Flaumina Untergasser wailed.

"Do you mind if I take liberties with your person?"

"Not at all. If you don't, I will."

She bore it as long as she could, for she could hardly believe her own eyes, and then she said:

"What on earth are you doing?"

"Cletterin' the dishes, Robert Poste's child."

"But surely you could do it much more easily with a little mop? A nice little mop with a handle. Cousin Judith ought to get you one. Why don't you ask her? It would get the dishes cleaner, and it would be so much quicker, too."

"I don't want a liddle mop wi' a handle. I've used a thorn twig these fifty years and more, and what was good enough then is good enough now. And I don't want to cletter the dishes more quickly, neither. It passes the time away, and takes me thoughts off my liddle wild bird."

"But," suggested the cunning Flora, remembering the conversation which had roused her that morning at dawn, "if you had a little mop and could wash the dishes more quickly, you could have more time in the cowshed with the dumb beasts."

— Stella Gibbons, *Cold Comfort Farm*

☞ For passages of one hundred or more words, indent and single-space the quotation and do not enclose it in quotation marks.

*The hand to kiss is the one you've
frightened away.*

∝❈ ?, !, and — go *inside* quotation marks when they belong to the quotation. Otherwise, they're on the outside looking in.

Too-Too asked, "Where's my tutu? Where's my tiara? Where are my roaring fans?"

Did Too-Too say "I can't find my luminous leg warmers"?

He was banging on the door and bellowing, "Open up, you adorable beast!"

Was I ever downcast when he said, "Let go of my pajamas, little darlin', and don't you cry or moan"!

How reassured I was, though, when he added, "Papa's gonna buy you a mockingbird"!

"Haven't you had enough time perusing that menu?" cried the waitress, grinding her teeth and stamping her ripple-soled feet.

∝❈ Remember this from the Comma chapter? No commas set off quoted material that is logically, musically, agreeably connected and at home with the general flow of the sentence.

"Relegate her to oblivion!" roared the queen as an occasional alternative to "Off with their heads!"

"Sod off" is a British version of our own indecorous dispatches and insulting farewells.

Presto Galooti, whose constituency included "the underestimated, the uninterested, and the uninvited," was the undeclared candidate of choice.

After rumors reached me that my last book was said to have been written by "a chic lesbian living in Rome," I decided I'd avoided this part of Italy too long, and swerved down here through Orvieto and a night on the floor above a hillside village bakery because a baby had arrived to occupy the guest room I'd been offered two years before.

꒰ Quotation marks are used (and should not be overused) to indicate an original, ironic, or unusual turn of phrase or nomenclature. Similarly, doubt or skepticism can be cast on others' words through this selective highlighting.

> They decided to adopt a "wait and see" attitude toward these new developments, and to look the other way.

> He said that for some *other* Christmas he'd give me a guide to safe sex with satyrs and centaurs, and a "going-places rocking horse."

꒰ Single quotation marks enclose a quotation within a quotation. Keep track, close them all, and see that punctuation is placed within the set to which it belongs.

> "Anyone care to hazard a guess at what 'spraggle upon waggle' means?" asked Jacob Other of his cat-eyed coeds.

> "How you managed to take Chaucer's 'The Parlement of Foules' and render it into a modern French that sounds so decisively and idiotically like Middle English is a marvel of verbal buffoonery I will never be able to fathom or forget."   *—Doomed*

> "A babel broke out, in which Aunt Ada could dimly be discerned beating at everybody with the *Milk Producers' Weekly Bulletin and Cowkeepers' Guide,* and shrilly

screaming: 'I saw it . . . I saw it! I shall go mad . . . I can't bear it . . . There have always been Starkadders at Cold Comfort. I saw something nasty in the woodshed . . . something nasty . . . nasty . . . nasty . . .'"
— Stella Gibbons, *Cold Comfort Farm*

"'Yes, I'm labefying my crumpet with all these nigmenogs,' replies Theo volubly."
— Raymond Queneau, *The Bark Tree*

∞ Note that in quotes within quotes, a question mark or exclamation point sticks to the set of quotation marks enclosing the question or exclamation.

"And did you really leave? Was your 'too soon' in pursuit of Horvath's 'too late'?"   — *Doomed*

∞ Indirect quotes swim right along into the sentence, not set off by quotation marks.

The king got out the word all over his realm that the princess was in need of playmates.

The duchess later told the press that she had no regrets and no intention of leaving our sweet little town.

∞ Omit quotation marks after *so-called, known as,* and *called.*

That so-called mastodon can cut quite the dapper figure when an escort is required.

Mandy, also known as Amaranthia, is taking her husband to the morgue.

They're roaring off to his laying-out on a motorcycle called Caliban.

꒰✤ Quoted poetry should be centered between the left and right margins and single-spaced, without quotation marks.

> For the Cherub Cat is a term of the Angel Tiger.
> For he has the subtlety and hissing of a serpent,
>   which in goodness he suppresses.
> For he will not do destruction, if he is well-fed, nei-
>   ther will he spit without provocation.
> For he purrs in thankfulness, when God tells him he's
>   a good Cat.
> — Christopher Smart

> Left to herself, the serpent now began
> To change; her elfin blood in madness ran,
> Her mouth foam'd, and the grass, therewith besprent,
> Wither'd at dew so sweet and virulent;
> Her eyes in torture fix'd, and anguish drear,
> Hot, glaz'd, and wide, with lid-lashes all sear,
> Flash'd phosphor and sharp sparks, without one
>   cooling tear.
> The colours all inflam'd throughout her train,
> She writh'd about, convuls'd with scarlet pain:
> A deep volcanian yellow took the place
> Of all her milder-mooned body's grace;
> And, as the lava ravishes the mead,
> Spoilt all her silver mail, and golden brede;
> Made gloom of all her frecklings, streaks and bars,
> Eclips'd her crescents, and lick'd up her stars:
> So that, in moments few, she was undrest,
> Of all her sapphires, greens, and amethyst,
> And rubious-argent: of all these bereft,
> Nothing but pain and ugliness were left.
> — John Keats

◒✤ Short quotations from poems may be written with the rest of the running text, with quotation marks enclosing them and with slashes between the lines.

> John Keats's "Lamia" continues: "And soon his eyes had drunk her beauty up, / Leaving no drop in the bewildering cup, / And still the cup was full, — while he, afraid / Lest she should vanish . . ."

> Christopher Smart further catalogues the virtues of his cat, Jeoffry: "For he can spraggle upon waggle at the word of command. / For he can jump from an eminence into his master's bosom."

◒✤ Quotation marks enclose the titles of short stories and poems, essays, articles, television and radio programs, songs and other short musical compositions. Periods and commas go inside quotation marks even when they are not part of the title.

> The cyclical nature of existence was revealed to her in half-hour snatches of "As the World Churns," a soap opera about biodegradable triangles and the proper uses of centrifugal force.

> "We Had a Dustbowl Love" was number one on the country-and-western charts for three weeks, giving way, in the fourth week of April, to "Josie, Is It True That You've Grown Hotter Than Your Tears?"

> I wish some deus ex machina would come along and slap some snazzy dénouement on my fate. (But the deus ex machina was at that moment reposing in a painting at the Musée d'Orsay — "Deus ex machina faisant

comme chez lui dans la baignoire" [Deus ex machina making himself at home in the bathtub].)

Heidi and Gabriel attended a sculpture exhibit of narcissism at play and asleep: a camera sitting before a beveled mirror taking picture after picture of itself in a ghostly little boudoir; and then a coffin with the inside of its lid a full-length mirror shining a reflection back at the unblinking corpse — "Beauty Rest," it's called.

Whose version of "Tutti-Frutti" packs the most wallop — Elvis's or Little Richard's?

The fourth chapter, "Comb," drags us through a mermaid's ablutions, an overgrown childhood in Cornwall, the Vikings at bedtime, and a treatment for chapped hands in which lamb chops figure significantly.

The lyrics to "Red Socks Beneath Black Piano: Play Me Some Blue Notes, Baby" are simple and straightforward enough; the sartorial details are not. The situation is just the reverse with Jean-Jacques Passera's homage to the American West, "Long Legs in the Eagle Cafe."

I have searched my book on Bosch for the image of a dancing clock I could have sworn ticked and jigged in "The Garden of Earthly Delights," but all I noticed in the way of time was that everyone was wearing watches on chains or on their wrists.

The premiere performance of "Vermeer Nocturne" included a maiden in the timpani section sloshing cream in a large pink pitcher, and a delicately lighted window through which the conductor waved his baton.

We went to a performance of "Das Knaben Wunderhorn" conducted by a Chicago cop.

She kept herself company through part of that insomniac night with a short story called "The Mauled Scribe."

Italics

SOME OF US are still in limbo between the typewriter and the computer, gradually realizing that italics are at our beckoning and then taking full pleasure in italicizing where we once underlined. During our courtship of these new keys and shapes, we may be wildly inconsistent, using both underlining and italics, with no logic to our choices, before succumbing totally to the slanting script. If I want to emphasize a joy or imprecation, underlining still feels the more effective, emphatic way to express it—but I could grow out of this attachment someday. Computers also give us the option of drawing attention to a word or phrase by choosing a different font, or size, or by selecting **bold.** And let's not forget our hands: writing by hand gives us further options for stressing and marking our words.

The dilemmas don't end here! Facing our own inconsistencies are those of the outside world, others' print and prose. Books more often use italics with titles, whereas newspapers and magazines may in some instances use quotation marks and roman type.

Simplicity and clarity tell me to use italics throughout this chapter, but you will see it swerving recklessly from one notation to another, whether or not I'm given a free hand.

⊃❧ The titles of books, movies, plays, and musical productions are *italicized* or underlined.

> *Ruffians in Chintz* went on to unabashed notoriety when it toured the hinterlands.
>
> Peter Sellars's production of *Così Fan Tutte* really takes the cake.
>
> Handel's *Israel in Egypt* calls me back to earth.
>
> The Agony and the Iniquity traces the tribulations of seven unnoticed heroes from the lower depths.
>
> *King Creole* was hands down Elvis's finest film performance; it lives on as testimony to both the ruination and the myth.
>
> Hiding behind a twofold double in *Hopscotch*, behind the bibliophile-discoverer in *The Name of the Rose*, and behind the *a posteriori* lexicographer in *Dictionary of the Khazars*, always subordinating their authorship to fiction, these authors actually succeed in strengthening their presence in their books.
>
> — Silvia Monrós-Stojaković

⊃❧ The titles of book-length poems are also italicized.

> Charles Simic's *White*   Milton's *Paradise Lost*
> Derek Walcott's *Omeros*   *The Divine Comedy*
>
> Chaucer, surprised at the tenderness he felt for his unfaithful heroine, cried into several handkerchiefs while writing Troilus and Criseyde.

William Carlos Williams's *Paterson* took on a theatrical cast in Ann Wilson's capable hands.

With no note or foreshadowing of her gift, Silvia sent me Njegoš's *The Ray of the Microcosm,* the more mystical of the poet/bishop/prince's celebrated epic poems.

ꙩ❧ The names of ships, aircraft, and spacecraft are *italicized* or <u>underlined</u>.

On this river alone we have three showboats — the *Plata*, the *Drina,* and the *Santa Fanina* — featuring tangos, kolos, and belly dance.

The good ship <u>Lollipop</u> leaves from the dock for the dentist's at ten o'clock.

The *Tinta*, the *Zebra,* and the *Scarlatina* are part of the fancifully painted maritime collection in a short film commonly shown with *Yellow Submarine.*

ꙩ❧ Italics bring emphasis when you wish to stress a single word, phrase, or expression — adding volume, weight, heat, shrillness, threat, or frustration at not being understood — and that's just the beginning of the reasons you might underscore or italicize.

♦ for ironic or vainglorious emphasis:

"You look ravishing."

"Oh, I wouldn't put it <u>that</u> mildly."

♦ for plaintive, heart-rending emphasis:

Would the endorphins *never* come?

Then where *was* I, if not in the wrong?

I wish people wouldn't say "Excuse me" when I *want* them to step on my feet.

I wish people wouldn't say "Excuse me" when I <u>want</u> them to step on my feet.

- for menace or boasting:

  I've got a free hand and can move *anything* with it.

- for unrequited platonic love:

  "Get your mind <u>off</u> me!"

- for special effect in social repartee:

  "Yes, well, I tell *everyone* things I wouldn't tell anyone else."

  That just really takes the frosting *off* the cake!

❧ Underline words, letters, figures, and symbols referred to as such.

  The *g* in lagniappe is a slide.

  Concatenations on the letter *t,* beginning with the missing teacups.
  — from a sliver of *The Glass Shoe*

  The word *lagniappe* communicates the special Creole idiom of generosity mixed with surprise.

  Stella Kirkenlied, at the labyrinth colloquy, defined *paranoia* as "self-aggrandizement with a twist."

  In his lecture on Kafka's "The Metamorphosis," Nabokov invented a new verb, *flimmering,* to describe Gregor Samsa's locomotion once he'd become a beetle.

❧ Words and phrases from other languages that slowly find their places in English are initially italicized to indicate that they're still not always with us — even appearing in italics in the dictionary. Many foreign expressions are sooner or later fully embraced, the italics lifted, the accent marks either dropped or retained — yet another degree of the adoption process. The following sentences are improbable examples of these various stages.

"Oh, baby, you are my *plus que parfait!*"

"Got time for a little *dolce far niente,* Timofey?" Nadia asked her paramour with eternity on his hands.

ↄ❧ As with other words of love from French, paramour has long been beyond the italics phase; the Italian *dolce far niente,* "sweet to do nothing," may take longer, as we become increasingly estranged from the delicious inactivity that this expression describes.

He's persona non grata, and non compos mentis besides.

The Transitive Vampire is the *ne plus ultra* of them all.

Alice im Wunderbar is a pub in Little Bavaria, Blegue, where English is the lingua franca.

Dvořák's music, from the symphonic to the chamber to the terpsichorean, takes its Slavic sparks and rhythms, its exotic *je ne sais quoi,* and even its back-in-the-old-starched-collars-and-socks-of-the-Austro-Hungarian-Empire nostalgia from such Czech folk dances as the *furiant,* polka, *skocná* (a reel), and a slow waltz, the *sousedska,* and the *dumka* (originally from Ukraine).

That *bildungsroman* par excellence is enjoying quite a *succès d'estime.*

Thanks to Youssou N'Dour, the *mbalax* is here to stay.

Tarantula's got her heart set on a ménage à trois with Rosie and Nimrod.

We started out with an *amuse-gueule* of jumping snails

and proceeded through a *salade composée* before the fireworks.

I crawled into my *schmatte* and stuck my foot through the door.

We went to the *hôtel de ville* to register our *concubinage*.

Weltschmerz didn't give our romance a flair for long; it soon gave way to bonhomie and décolletage.

Amplochacha has become the very *fons et origo* of enlightened approaches to twists of fate.

I've got a free hand and can move <u>anything</u> with it.

Parentheses

PARENTHESES pal around in pairs to enact their literal meaning taken from the Greek: a putting in beside. They make for a softer interruption than the abrupt snapping or darting that dashes do, and they find many situations where they feel at home. But don't let them move in on you so that the real message ducks for cover between them rather than proudly taking its place in the out-there-for-everyone-to-see-main-street of the sentence, or you'll be accused of being coy, or annoying, or sophomoric (and we know how abhorrent that would be!). Still, the parentheses do enticingly embrace extra material of all sorts, from unwelcome long-winded digressions to amusing crisp asides; wisecracks and other comments; and amplification or explanation of the sentence in which the parenthetical prose is ensconced.

> I was in a coma yesterday (well, figuratively speaking) from two weeks of trust-busting litigation and grieving for my beloved Bosoxia.

> She arrived late (just as well) and put mud in their vitriol.

He's probably out there (in the waiting room)
sitting in his own lap.

To postpone the inevitable fracas for which they had come, Rosie, Nimrod, and assorted guests stuck to less touchy topics (renku, heliotropes, Balanchine) 'til Loona gave the incendiary wink.

As the lady of the house descended the staircase, the nude (one of her earlier amours) hung in an alcove on the *rez-de-chaussée* came crashing to the floor.

Sola (whose full given name is Solamente la Noche) writes in Spanish when she's excited and in English as a follow-up to be sure she'll have her way.

Vasily said that they (those guys in the troika) are campaigning for fakery in furs.

He's probably out there (in the waiting room) sitting in his own lap.

The neighbors in this sylvan, sometime paradise are clobbering each other, and her toothless face is starting to rend my shirt (very Gothic), so I think I'll go mail this at the post office and get back to those French tangles of sensuous words.

Would they *ever* stop fighting (those mean spirited nationalists) and start making beautiful buttons and films again?

The man in the red cape put on Mozart's Divertimento in D Major (K. 136), rummaged around in his sewing basket for a spool of scarlet thread, made a double *Kaffee mit Schlag,* and, as Saint Martin gamboled about in the melodic fields, addressed himself to the fraying matter of his hood.

We took a tortuous route (through small talk, double-entendres, a few drinks, and some polite evasions) to arrive at a state of intimacy where we pleasantly admired our bodies.

✺ Comments introduced by *e.g., i.e., namely, see, see also, that is,* and *viz,* are enclosed when they break the continuity of the sentence.

A pack of her relatives (namely, Aunt Toosla, Uncle Ladislas, Aunt Kamila, and Uncle Laslo, and their eight children from the ages of three to eleven) stood on her veranda with sunscreen, tennis rackets, pillows, alarm clocks, and a promissory note from a queen in Blegue.

✺ Parentheses go around numbers or letters listing items in a series that are part of a running text.

Chapman thought that Karen Snow-Mariée's "The Wretch of Lugubria" suffered from (1) pretentiousness, (2) pessimism, and (3) an effulgence of narrators.

✺ In legal documents, numbers that are first spelled out are followed, for clarity, by numerals clutched between parentheses.

The fifty million (50,000,000) dahlias were delivered in a droshky and deposited with no word of their provenance.

✺ When a question mark or exclamation point belongs to a shout, surprise, or otherwise excited comment within a parenthetical musing, it stays inside the parentheses, close to the words involved.

We took a tortuous route (through small talk, double-entendres, a few drinks, and some polite evasions) to arrive at a state of intimacy where we pleasantly admired our bodies.

He called her Bambi (or was it Jacaranda?) when no one else was listening.

You'll go places! You'll be all over the Big Picture! In a blazing trail of broken glass! Mark my words! Glory awaits you with flashing lights and scratchy clothes! (Believe me, I know what I'm talking about!) You'll soon be talking back to a sphinx on some talk show and baring your soul like a starlet!

If you'll let the cat out of his pajamas, I'll show you what else he dragged in. (Actually, the cat had made off with his tongue and was batting it about in a corner of the bedroom!)

⋊✤ At times, a lone parenthetical ? or ! rears its head in a sentence to interject doubt, surprise, or otherwise call attention editorially to a word choice or outrageous statement.

The runner-up in the war of the roses was a new hybrid from Amplochacha called Greetings to Le Corbusier (?), or maybe it was Le Courvoisier.

Creeping along our menu on his fingers, Imbroglio, our waiter that evening, suggested the capon braised in white whine (!) and the empirical sausages.

⋊✤ A parenthetical sentence within another sentence does not begin with a capital letter nor end with a period. A freestanding parenthetical sentence between two other sentences, though, requires a capital letter and a period.

The dessert course offered us insuperable quandaries (well, what would *you* say to stuffed shirts baked in Alaska, or looking-glass lace made from hot tatted

I took my time getting close to him (in an utter stupor, I spent half an hour dressing while he waited for me below) and even longer to tell him my name.

collars and rolled cream?), so we left with our hearts
in our throats and uncommon coins in our reticules.

I took my time getting close to him (in an utter stupor,
I spent half an hour dressing while he waited for me
below) and even longer to tell him my name.

We had finished our Irish coffee. (We had plenty of
time, we thought, to get to the theater.) We wanted to
prolong that moment past fulfillment, bedtime, and
death.

Brackets

⊃❧ Brackets are used to enclose editorial remarks or words inserted as explanation within a direct quotation.

"That prima donna [Too-Too LaBlanca] is but a pirouette away from her bedbugs and weasels," concluded Sola's merciless review.

"Nobody recognized her [the defenestrated duchess] when she resurfaced in Paris as a gypsy soprano on fire with a strange new accent and a repertoire of trills, ululations, and flashing eyes."

"Her tongue scalded from the cup of cocoa and her mind filled with terrors of the tale she had just laid aside ["The Mauled Scribe"], she tossed fitfully among the bedclothes while mummies masquerading as hieroglyphs packed her, lace nightie and all, into the silt of the riverbank and spelled out her destiny in an awkward performance of calisthenics as her eyes peeped in fright from the mud."

The streets rollicked with jubiliant [sic] voters extolling their winning candidate, Simca Moonbach.

♦ 121 ♦

✺ Brackets enclose the remark *sic* to indicate unusual or whimsical spellings and genuine errors in quoted material.

"The streets rollicked with jubiliant [*sic*] voters extolling their winning candidate, Simca Moonbach."

Her epistolary torrent ended, "Roofully [*sic*] yours, Laurinda T. Moostracht."

"When we play dress grownup at alla ludo poker you'll be happnessised [*sic*] to feel how fetching I can look in clinagrounds."

— James Joyce, *Finnegans Wake*

The invitation "for drinks and relapsation [*sic*]" went out to all the usual "drinks and humiliations riffraff of Adriadne auf (Opening Nacht [*sic*]) SoHo."

☞ Brackets set themselves off just fine without additional punctuation. If the material within the brackets requires internal punctuation, add the commas, colons, semicolons where they belong, but commas are not needed to break the sentence and make way for the brackets.

✺ Brackets are used to enclose stage directions.

LOONA [*pacing hypnotically*]: How long, how long must I wait?

MALVOLIO [*snapping his yellow garters*]: You don't say!

NADIA [*still doing her nails*]: Cat got your tongue, Timofey?

✺ Brackets are not glorified or horrified parentheses. They usually set off material that is independent of the sentence

LOONA [pacing hypnotically]: *How long, how long must I wait?*

in which they rear their scholarly little heads, and they are used much more frequently in academic writing than in literary, casual, affectionate prose (drama's the one exception). Brackets are, however, sometimes used for parenthetical material within parentheses:

"You're not mad?" she asked (she was twirling her whistle in her right hand [it looked like her wolf had been chewing on it or using it to call down the moon] and waving her toe [the enormous one I told you about] back and forth over the ottoman I'd repeatedly asked her to treat with more respect), obviously hoping to delay my response, since she knew all along what it would be.

꘎ Brackets also set off phrases bearing information or instructions.

[Continued on page 268]

[To be continued]

[Eat your cookie before proceeding to the dénouement]

The
Slash/Bar/Virgule/
Diagonal/Separatrix

A TILTED perpendicular, an ambivalent floorwalker, the slash/virgule/bar/separatrix offers alternatives, and when needed accompanies coordinate conjunctions as their chaperon. This sidekicking factotum also adds its angle to measurements, and further ennobles itself by marking the end of a line of quoted poetry that appears in the midst of other text.

❧ The slash separates alternatives that may exist simultaneously in one person/place/thing/notion, or are offered up as possible choices. This is waffling territory at its most sublime! And why not, since this punctuation mark can't settle on one name for itself, but keeps its options open.

The multi-mediac Surrealists are alluring company for the virgule, which we can send sliding through their manifestoes and curricula vitae among collaborations, world wars, multiple nationalities, serial lovers and spouses, emigrations, and fallings-out.

The English-born writer/painter/photographer
Leonora Carrington led a land/water life/existence

and wrote "The Debutante" about a hyena that is captured by a resourceful rebel and is all tricked out in dress and mask to attend the ball in the heroine's place.

The Dadaist/Surrealist Hans/Jean Arp, from Alsace-Lorraine (hence the binational given name changing with the landscape and native tongue), was a sculptor/poet/paper cutter whose shapes showed eyes their home.

The immense, unmistakable eyes of Gala Eluard/Dali greeted the crowd filing in through the first spectacles of "Paul Eluard et ses amis peintres" in fall/winter 82/83 at the Pompidou Center.

✂ Here are some other realms for alternatives/choices where the slash has lured us to stray.

She has this phobia/quirk/fatal flaw that attaches itself to telephones — or pianos if they're around.

Each of the scullions was to keep his/her fingers out of the trifle, and his/her eyes on the flies.

The gangsters/rats were often kind to widows/widowers, and to bambinos in overalls.

The girl/boy scouts couldn't have cared less about lepidopterology, but were eager for any outings in the woods.

Does this ingénue/kangaroo drive a jeep and/or carry her eventual young ones in a pouch?

We hit the asphalt/tarmac with flying colors and wings aflame with desire.

Well, you can just tell that he-/she-monster to shut his/her trap and come into the parlor for scones.

And how long do you suppose/expect this light house-keeping/concubinage will last?

Ladies and gentlemen, our distempered *Klavierstücker* will now humor you out of the evening's earlier dissonance by playing your requests on the piano/harpsichord and plucking the lyre/harpoon.

And then, after he punctuated me on the upstroke, he frawndled and galooted my ovations and suggested a postpunctual snack/snooze at the Fons et Origo in Blue.

The wildebeest, Schlaffenfuss's pet mannequin, was lithe and supple, when not actually bounding, on the runway, and weighed in at 50 kg/110 lb.

❧ As we saw through Gala Eluard/Dali's eyes above, the slash separates elements in a timespan.

the March/April issue of *De Gustibus*

1985/86 academic year

❧ The slash keeps coordinate conjunctions apart when words aren't linking them, as is usually the case in sentences.

This neither/nor sandwich of negation you're offering me is hardly one for the road.

It's an either/or kind of Catch-22 with no hope for the likes of you/us.

❧ The slash/bar/virgule often represents *per,* as in *miles per hour, feet per second.*

The borzoi/Russian greyhound (80 km/hr) was destined to become, with Olja, the handsomest couple in town.

*Does this ingénue/kangaroo drive a jeep and/or carry her
eventual young ones in a pouch?*

That hallucinogen can be had on the street in Blegue for $400/oz; the odd dealer in Louvelandia can be talked down to $250/oz.

This mouse-powered cement truck gets 5 miles/gallon when the cat's away.

Ↄ❦ The slash is also used to distinguish phonemes and phonetic transcription.

/c/ as in camouflage

/g/ as in frangipani

/ll/ as in llama

Ↄ❦ When lines of poetry are written out in text, slashes step right in to show where the lines actually break.

"family ties cross the currents / into a net and cups of represso / you think you've found this sweet hotel / rooms come with a bang and a whisper"

"Icebox Renku" lingers with lust and incense in one of those rooms: "second thoughts yapping at / their heels or the maid / clapping black galoshes."

The

Apostrophe

⁊❧ One of the apostrophe's most legitimate activities is showing possession.

A woman's place is on the roam.

Parvenuing into the duchess's arms were many more than one ringleted *valet de chambre* and an inexperienced worthless lout.

a mother's nightmare

Too-Too's tutu

Jacaranda's fichu

⁊❧ In forming the possessive singular of phrases and expressions used as compound nouns, the last word of the compound gets an apostrophe *s*.

Henry IV's statue in Place Dauphine is pregnant with Napoleon.

The Countess of Troo's ocelot is sharpening its claws on the tapestry again.

Sir Gallimauf complimented Moostracht Senior on his *valet de chambre's* fetching ringlets.

❧ The apostrophe is attached to the *last* word in a hyphenated noun, and, while we're in this region, we'll visit some other compounds.

> Her sister-in-law's bangles alternated with Gabor's unaccompanied cello suites.
>
> the deus ex machina's bath water
>
> a persona non grata's face
>
> his mother-in-law's cookies
>
> that white-collar worker's grievances

Note too:

> someone else's high heels
>
> William Least Heat-Moon's *Blue Highways*
>
> Duchess Ilona's maid-in-waiting's handkerchief

❧ If two or more nouns possess something together, only the last noun carries the apostrophe.

> Jean-Pierre and Alyosha's baggage
>
> Nimbo and Laurinda's betrothal
>
> Ilona and Ivan's country
>
> Room service arrived with Rosie and Nimrod's crustaceans.
>
> Laurinda and Nimbo's honeymoon was eclipsed by the revolution in Lavukistan.
>
> Anjula and Alyosha's common language ran out of hyperbole.

a mother's nightmare

🜂 When the possession is not shared, this must be distinguished by the use of separate apostrophes and *s*'s.

> Todor did Anjula's and Alyosha's hair.
>
> The nannies' and milkmaids' lexicons were in for a major overhaul.
>
> Cortázar and Silva's collaboration (together)
>
> Cortázar's and Silva's memories (separate, even if stirred by the same maté)
>
> Aunt Toosla's and Uncle Ladislas's backhands
>
> Aunt Kamila and Uncle Laslo's homeland

🜂 Plural nouns ending in *s* become possessive with the addition of an apostrophe. For plurals not ending with an *s*, an apostrophe and *s* are often needed to form the possessive.

> the goats' picnic in the haberdashery
>
> those mastodons' beautiful manners
>
> the vampires' fear of white-collar workers
>
> the zebras' stripes
>
> the bouncers' suspenders
>
> the women's waistlines and willfulness
>
> the children's hyperkinesia

🜂 A noun modifying a gerund is usually in the possessive case.

> Anjula's riding off into the sunset was witnessed only by a herd of elk.

🜂 For some possessions and other interactions, you will find an *of* phrase most obliging.

⋙ The object of an action takes an *of* phrase, not the possessive case.

> the gagging and binding of Sir Gallimauf's mechanic
>
> the defenestration of Duchess Ilona
>
> the assassination of Robert Kennedy
>
> the fatal drugging of Marilyn Monroe

⋙ An inanimate object takes possession of things with an *of* phrase. This is true of qualities, and abstract nouns, too, most of the time.

> the sea of stories the howls of the wolves
>
> the soul of discretion the way of the world
>
> the birth of the bustle the ends of the earth
>
> a daze of gratitude the edge of the night
>
> the blaze of the moon

> The beatification of Saint Fracas came off with only one slight hitch.

> NOT: my affections' object
>
> BUT: the object of my affections

⋙ Running almost rampant through our language are idiomatic expressions referring to time, space, money, and more intimate qualities that are written with an apostrophe *s*.

> a hard day's night
>
> a year's wages
>
> twenty bucks' worth
>
> the evening's winnings
>
> my heart's desire
>
> a week's worth of salt in his sweat and tears

a crow's flight to the north

her wit's end

✺ Although possessive personal and interrogative pronouns go apostrophe free (*its, hers, his, ours, yours, theirs,
whose*), possessive indefinite pronouns require them:
anyone's, somebody's, someone else's, each other's, everyone's.

> Whose are those shoes?
>
> They're not his or hers; they're Gaby's, and no one
> else should try to step into them.
>
> Each one's red licorice whip lost its vigor in the torrid
> heat.
>
> Somebody's perturbation is catching on throughout
> the land.
>
> Anyone's laughing out of place will excite the master's
> indignation.

✺ No apostrophe enters into arrangements to show the
plural of proper nouns.

> Happy birthday to Miranda, from the Gallimaufs.
>
> The Raduloviches had us over for *slotko*, iced tea, and
> cards.

✺ Apostrophes are used to form the past participle of certain words in occasional use — or your own — concocted
out of nouns.

> Nimbo O.K.'d the extravagant check drawn on an
> Azurikoan bank.
>
> Allegro non Troppo was K.O.'d when he strayed into
> hostile territory.

A woman's place is on the roam.

Nicaragua was Sandinista'd when Julio first arrived.

He had me Bach'd into a corner with his thumping, ill-tempered clavier.

She likes to keep her studio fully *mbalax'd* when she springs into her words.

๐෴ An apostrophe stands in for numbers omitted, when, for instance, we know which century is meant.

> the class of '68
>
> toward the end of '82
>
> not far into '93

๐෴ *It's* is the contraction of *it is*.

> It's humanly impossible.

๐෴ Without the apostrophe, *its* is the possessive of *it*.

> What's that bauble in its beak?
>
> I was too busy averring my culinary prejudices to notice the sheep's head clacking its teeth on his plate.

๐෴ The apostrophe moves in to cover for a letter (or letters) that's been dropped in contractions, which just happened with *that has*, and in colloquial speech that adds so much charm to the musical scene, as in these lyrics from the country 'n' western (there's another one! two!) song cycle *Cowboys and Lingerie*.

> Honey, yer bra strap's been slitherin' down yer shoulder since you stopped yer cheatin' ways.
>
> Baby, you bin good to me
> an' my silken underthings.

You never lost one sock o' mine,
but Ah cain't stand yer anfractuous ways.

You put my heart through the wringer,
I'm hangin' it out on the line.

☛ A footnote, wearin' a cowboy boot: These lyrics are sung in an amphitheater with clotheslines draped over the stage and out into the audience. Most of the time the cowboys are washing their silk teddies and underpants studded with red rhinestone hearts and rhinestone-eyed cows, and hanging them to dry.

Cowboys aren't the only ones to drop vowels and consonants here and there. The following scene of begrudging social grace is far from the yuccas and cacti.

What'm I s'posed to do—sit on the edge of my chair and bark rapturously while you regale me with cheap verbal postcards of your trip across Blegue?

Cowboys have this much in common with the English romantics, who also dropped vowels from their verses, for the sake of the scan, as Keats does here, in "Lamia."

Thus gentle Lamia judg'd, and judg'd aright,
That Lycius could not love in half a fright,
So threw the goddess off, and won his heart
More pleasantly by playing woman's part,
With no more awe than what her beauty gave,
That, while it smote, still guaranteed to save.

The apostrophe used in this way signals antiquated diction, should you strive for such an effect.

O Spring, you are gaudy and bawdy in your perfum'd
Petal'd skirts, your buzzing, trilling refrains!

Ellipses

. . . AS I WAS SAYING, ellipses come in threes and fours, and each collection of periods has its function in indicating omitted words.

○✦ Three dots stand for an omission within or at the beginning of a sentence. The first sentence begins with an omission, and the third sentence contains ellipses to indicate missing words.

". . . and so his gnarled hand held on to her raincoat long after she'd given him the slip."

"If it was the budding ballerina who answered the door, she was wearing her raincoat because either the roof was leaking on a rainy day or she had been pirouetting about the house in her makeshift tutu and flung on the first garment her hand fell upon in a dark closet modesty compelled her to open at the sound of the bum's rap."

"If . . . the budding ballerina . . . answered the door, she was wearing her raincoat because . . . she had

been pirouetting . . . in her makeshift tutu and flung
on the first garment her hand fell upon . . . at the
sound of the bum's rap."

✣ In order to make more sense of the quoted material or to
indicate what has been omitted, commas or other punctuation may aptly appear on the relevant side of the
three ellipsis dots.

". . . and furthermore, I have no use for your dirty
politics, your coy mannerisms, . . . your deadening
monologues, . . . and your snarls of self-righteousness
that have endeared you to your pathetic followers."

✣ Compare this passage of Gogol's "The Nose" to the abbreviated version below it.

"I won't even listen to you! Do you really imagine
that I'll allow a cut-off nose to remain in my place,
you old crumb! All you do is strop your damn razor,
and when it comes to your duties, you're no good.
You stupid, lousy, skirt-chasing scum! So you want
me to get into trouble with the police for your sake? Is
that it, you dirty mug? You're a stupid log, you know.
Get it out of here. Do what you like with it, you hear
me, but don't let me ever see it here again."

"I won't even listen to you! Do you really imagine that
I'll allow a cut-off nose to remain in my place . . . !
All you do is strop your damn razor. . . .
You're a stupid log, you know. . . . Don't let me ever
see it here again."

☞ But don't take words out of context or change the
sense of the passage:

"I . . . even listen to you! . . . I'll allow a cut-off nose to remain in my place. . . . Do what you like with it, . . . but . . . let me . . . see it here again."

⊃⬥ Four dots (a period followed by three spaced dots) are used to show omission of the final words of the quoted sentence, the first words of the following one, an entire sentence or more, or a complete paragraph or more. A question mark or exclamation mark in the original remains and is followed by the three dots of the ellipsis.

"A decidedly female fog lies upon the earth hereabouts, constantly rearranging her coiffure. . . . And night, my woman, is expected soon, with her many winking eyes."   — *Doomed*

". . . your face, which is soft, refreshing, the bloom of youth just bursting forth or beginning to fade. How I long to kiss it, or at least to know your name! . . . I can almost see your chest heaving gently and your eyelashes flapping as your eyes caress the page."

"Days like this give sight a rest and allow other senses to function more freely. . . . It was either raining or pretending to rain or not raining at all, yet still appearing to rain in a sense that only certain old Northern dialects can either express verbally or not express, but versionize, as it were, through the ghost of a sound produced by a drizzle in a haze of grateful rose shrubs."

— Vladimir Nabokov
Transparent Things

". . . the ground opened up at these words and we found ourselves in a dripping cavern with all sorts of gewgaws hanging out of its cracks. . . . But what happened after this is so dreadful that it would distress me to say any more."

— The Gingerbread Variations

"He was awakened at the creak of dawn by a flannel flapping sound. Although it had no knees to speak of, a long-sleeved nightgown with rows of roses climbing blue and white lattices knelt in the doorway waving its lace-cuffed arms and swaying from side to side to a rhythm he couldn't quite put his finger on, but which smacked of Africa. . . .

"As he soon discovered, the flannel nightgown was in fact a gospel singer, who regaled him with her sabbath repertoire until the first rays of daylight broke in on the shadows of that full-bodied voice, which disappeared into a laundry chute. This gave his silk dressing gown something to think about after he'd slammed the door on his breakfast of solitude and caught the tramway of travail. What sweet emotions those folds of flannel had evoked! No matter that the hands that might have been clapping were now rubbing the contralto over the washboard as its mouth filled up with soap and the hallelujahs caused large bubbles to burst in the sun. The silk dressing gown, which had never been immersed in such stuff in its life, nor submitted to an abrasive touch on its fine and many-colored threads, made sure the coast was clear before stepping into the hallway and entering a new life before the mirror of gyrations and fervor theretofore in its murkiest dreams unspun."

— "Closet Drama,"
Intimate Apparel

As we see in the passage above, no closing quotation mark is necessary following the end of a paragraph of quoted material that runs on to another paragraph; an opening quotation mark does, however, begin each subsequent quoted paragraph.

ɔɕ An ellipsis indicates that a listing, enumeration, or roll call goes on beyond the items given/named/stated.

> Cabbage, beets, vinegar . . . stir all the ingredients lustily while thinking of Chichikov, or, better yet, those charming Volga boatmen representing their beloved waterway at the Hotel Indigeau.
>
> At the starting shot, the horses jerked forward in all good speed — Mocha Java, Earl Grey, Friendly Fire, Northern Lights. . . .
>
> We were learning the wondĕrs ŏf the Serbian, Croatian, Slovenian tongues — *ć, c, š, z* . . .

ɔɕ Ellipses can be summoned forth to punctuate items in a series, implying that not all is being reported, just darting glimpses, scattered thoughts; you bet there's more to tell.

> Hair-raising exploits in perilous lands . . . trysts beneath the honeysuckle . . . forming a threesome with a dentist and his tango partner . . . languishing in mud and museums in the spas and cities of Europe . . . having twins and/or a political career . . . these were some of the futures she contemplated while finishing her baccalaureate at Amplochacha U.
>
> The duchess looked back on her midlife escapades . . . that handsome bounder who didn't know his way in

. . . trysts beneath the honeysuckle . . . forming a three-some with a dentist and his tango partner . . .

any world, the lap of luxury she left with him or the rougher one they tumbled into . . . that first night sleeping in a ditch beside a moonless road . . . howling forests and brigands with fans not even bothering to accost her . . . a strange new town where mastodons took dancing lessons and went to foreign films . . . her thoughts straying back to the deserted — and dessert-ed — duke backing into the fire as she bid him farewell. . . . Did he take up with a pack of tarts? or did he just finish the ones she'd left by the fireplace?

ɔ❀ To punctuate the end of a quotation that is deliberately incomplete as a sentence, three dots will suffice.

"I have never been to a masquerade ball. I do, how-ever, remember the pleasant sensation my hand expe-rienced when it picked up a mask. I have in mind a woman's black mask. Or rather, half mask.

"It was black on the outside and white on the in-side, and was much nicer from that, its reverse side. Those white satin impressions in place of nose and cheeks for some reason seemed to take on the shape of a smile, the smile of a beautiful young face.

"When you threw it, it fell on the table with an al-most imperceptible tap. It was lightness itself, ele-gance itself, love itself. It danced, it sang, it looked at you.

"There are perhaps few things so lovely as a mask. It was a woman, it was a Renoir, it was a dream; it was 'tomorrow,' it was 'probably,' it was 'in a moment, a moment, wait, in a moment . . .'"

— Yury Olesha
No Day Without a Line

Thanks

Scattered thanks over the years and distances to Cathy Romero, David Bromige, Jesus de la Ossa, Kay Turney, Carol Dunlop, and Julio Cortázar. My heart goes back to my first and only cowboy, Clint Smoot, whose lingerie is *not* in the Apostrophe chapter. Camilla Collins and Maia Gregory kept the wolves from the door so the wolf within could howl.

Jean-Jacques Passera provided the inside dope on Henry IV and Napoleon. My esteemed colleague, Jacques Drillon, kept me on my toes and off Too-Too LaBlanca's. Harvey Sachs made me mindful of musical faux pas.

At several stages Maureen Jung's organizational and WorkPerfect finesse kept things moving, but mostly in place. With gleaming swiftness and comprehension, Irene Bogdanoff Romo finishingly touched the images that were rustling the pages as they awakened.

Larry Cooper made the usual ordeal of manuscript editing a pleasure. My editor Cindy Spiegel brought a verbal felicity and lilting speed to this production, at times resembling the gazelles you'll often see headed for the hyphens and dashes.

The collage about hands and letters face-up I made for Sylvia Monrós-Stojaković. Jann Donnenwirth added her presence and wisdom, Zoë her mute tolerance. I pause to honor Caton of Rue Gassendi and Flanelle of Rue Martel, with their variations on Mandelstam's literary fur coat.

Dover Publications is a treasured, ceaseless source of images. Linda Parker-Guenzel and Fred Guenzel contributed their collection, too, along with unflagging interest.

Nick Bantock's lighthouse is visiting from Ta Fin. Olja Ivanjicki stepped off a page of *Knjiga o Olji* (Književne Novine, Beograd, 1984). Barrie Maguire let loose his star-striped ikon with polished toenails for her political triumph in Brackets. The river spirit wearing my own dress is by Rastislav Mrazovac.

The Disheveled Dictionary

A Curious Caper
Through Our Sumptuous Lexicon

"Entertaining . . . ingenious . . . an eclectic collection of words."
— *Los Angeles Times Book Review*
A Los Angeles Times Best Book of the Year

With her signature cache of illustrations and flamboyantly gothic examples, Karen Elizabeth Gordon, "who has achieved cult status with her whimsical references, defines an array of daffy, delicious words" (*Library Journal*).

ISBN 0-618-38196-1 / $10.00